THE CORE VALUE EQUATION

THE

A FRAMEWORK TO DRIVE RESULTS,

CORE

CREATE LIMITLESS SCALE

VALUE

AND WIN THE WAR FOR TALENT

EQUATION

DARIUS MIRSHAHZADEH

LIONCREST
PUBLISHING

THE CORE VALUE EQUATION
*A Framework to Drive Results, Create Limitless
Scale and Win the War for Talent*

ISBN   978-1-5445-0672-2   *Hardcover*
      978-1-5445-0670-8   *Paperback*
      978-1-5445-0671-5   *Ebook*

This book is dedicated to my wife Maria and children, Rumi and Pablo.
You inspire me everyday to try to bring my best self to the world.

CONTENTS

INTRODUCTION

"I hate this company," I said to myself, sitting in the office in San Francisco. "I can't believe I created this."

This was in the spring of 2007. I had just spent the last four years creating the fortieth-fastest-growing private company in the United States with my twin brother. I had everything that I thought I had ever dreamed of. I was twenty-eight years old. I was the CEO of my own high-growth company. My company was on track to have our first year of revenue in excess of $10,000,000. I had 150 employees and growing. I had a seventeen-thousand-square-foot modern tech office space in the heart of San Francisco's SOMA district. I had created a monster, and I had just realized it.

Be careful what you wish for—because sometimes when you get it, it's not what you imagined it would be. I had always known I would be a CEO. My brother Mike and I had grown up watching our father be an entrepreneur, and we were always told that one day we, too, would run our own businesses. I had tried to drop out of college multiple times because I did not see the point of getting a degree; I was going to work for myself. My brother and

I had spent our childhood building businesses. From building a candy empire in the fourth grade, to door-to-door sales, to creating an events-promotion company in college, to building our first legitimate company at the age of twenty-five in San Francisco—having a normal job was never in the cards.

In 2003, when we founded Twin Capital Mortgage, the resources for twenty-something CEOs and founders were few and far between. In 2006, we had grown our company to roughly one hundred employees, and we were having growing pains like you would not believe. We had grown from a one-room two-hundred-square-foot office to seventeen thousand square feet of modern office space filled with twenty-somethings all trying to get rich in the mortgage industry. It was an exhilarating time, and we were learning every day what it meant to scale a business. We were making every mistake in the book. We cared deeply about building a great company. In June of 2006, I was lucky enough to be admitted into the prestigious Birthing of Giants (BOG) Entrepreneurial Masters Program at MIT. The program was started by Verne Harnish, the author of *Scaling Up* and *Mastering the Rockefeller Habits*. It was designed to help high-growth CEOs under the age of forty with scaling their businesses using cutting-edge best practices.

The program was two years long; it began in June 2006 and finished in June 2008, with three meetings: year one (June 2006), year two (June 2007), and year three (June 2008). I would come back each year with my head spinning, trying to implement what I had learned to build my business into a world-class organization. One of the first teachings at BOG was that our companies had to have core values. So, I designed a set of core values and "rolled them out" to my organization to let our team know what we stood for. As time went on, I noticed that a lot of the behavior I saw in the company did not align with what I believed the company stood for. It also did not align with the core values that I had rolled out. We had grown too fast and I had not done a good job of discovering, designing, and bringing the core values to life in my company. I basically had created the core values of the company, hung them on the wall, and then gone back to work. The core values were simply my beliefs on a piece of paper. (I now call these "words on paper," an idea we will explore later in the book.) I had not collaborated with my leadership team to discover what we truly stood for as an organization. I had not designed the core values to be user-friendly. I had not rolled them out properly to our team. I had basically done everything you could possibly do wrong if my goal was to create a core-value-driven organization. In short, I had failed.

The moment that solidified how big a failure I was came after my second year at BOG. I was walking into the Twin Capital office from our parking garage. There was a long hallway that took me from the garage into our office suite, and every day I would walk down that hallway and I would get excited, like how a performer or athlete feels just before they go on stage or enter the stadium for the big game. I would enter our large seventeen-thousand-square-foot bullpen, say good morning to our receptionist, and then head to my office, which had a large glass wall overlooking the entire sales floor.

This morning, I didn't go directly to my office. I walked over to our compliance desk to ask about a file we were having an issue with. There were two young guys working at the compliance desk. I approached one of them, named Brian.

"Hey, Brian. What's going on with the Smith file?"

"I dunno, man." Brian shrugged. "It's not my job."

And at that moment, I felt as if someone had hit me across the head with a baseball bat. Never in my wildest dreams could I have imagined answering a question like that—let alone to the CEO of the company. I was dumbstruck. And I was livid.

You see, it wasn't the fact that I felt disrespected as the CEO that offended me. It was the idea that I had created an organization that would allow someone who would find it acceptable to give this as an answer to be a part of the organization. I realized that I had created an organization that allowed for this kind of cultural mismatch.

This is one of those moments in my career that is seared into my brain. It was the moment I realized I had built a business that had people who probably did not share my company's core values. I saw my company in a new light—a patched-together Frankenstein. I had created a monster.

To say I was upset was an understatement. My response to Brian expressed my frustration at that moment:

"You know, Brian—whose job is it, then? Is it my job? I'm the CEO."

I walked away, disgusted and disappointed. But it was not disgust or disappointment in Brian. It was disgust and disappointment in myself. I had finally built this company that I had dreamed of since I was a child, and it was not something I was proud of.

Back in my office, sitting in my chair, I said to myself, "I hate this company. I can't believe I created this." I looked out through that large glass wall, to the buzzing sales floor. Then I said, "And it's all my fault."

This book is written for all the leaders out there looking to truly build a core-value-driven organization. My definition of a core-value-driven organization is where the values are lived consistently, and where people know and act based on the organization's values. It is a place where people hold one another accountable to these common set of values above all else. Lastly a core-value-driven organization is one where you and your team know the core values off the top of your head. If this is not the case for your company, then you have just cracked open the right book.

This book will solve three of the biggest pain points companies and CEOs face in today's business world:

1. How do you create the ultimate decision-making engine for your organization, which will lead your organization to spectacular results that you can consistently control from the highest levels of the organization?
2. How can you create an invisible manager that sits next to every team member in your organization? This manager will hold every team member accountable to a common set of beliefs, will participate in every action and every outcome, and will do so without you hiring a single person to do it. This is what I call "invisible scale," and it is what I believe to be the most powerful tool for scale that an organization can possess.
3. How can you truly win in the war of talent acquisition? This book will teach you how to recruit and support an army of die-hard team members who speak the same language,

create consistent results, and believe the same beliefs that you, as a CEO and founder, live by in your organization day in and day out.

I have spent the greater part of the last twenty years building high-growth companies from startup to hundreds of employees. Over the span of the last two decades, I have learned what it takes to start from nothing and grow my companies exponentially, generating over $1,000,000,000 in top-line revenue, creating nationally recognized Best Places to Work, building nationally recognized cultures, being recognized as one of the top CEOs in the United States, and, most importantly, learning how to build and scale a core-value-driven organization from zero to one thousand employees. I have learned by making *every* mistake in the book. Throw out all the notions you have on how to build a core-value-driven organization. Strap on your seat belt and get ready for a wild and bumpy ride.

PART 1

CHAPTER 1

YOUR COMPANY HAS NO CORE VALUES

Wow, I am a loser.

This was the thought that crossed my mind as I sat down. It was 2008 and year three of the coveted BOG program at MIT, and I was in a peer-to-peer workshop led by the co-CEOs of Nurse Next Door, Ken Sim and John DeHart. Ken and John had built Nurse Next Door into one of the most admired companies in Canada. They had done so by creating a company that thrived on its core values. Today, they were testing all sixty of us at BOG to see if we had effectively rolled out the core values in our companies.

"Please stand up if your company has core values," Ken says.

We all stood up.

"Please stay standing up," John says, "if you know the core values of your company and can say them off the top of your head."

Out of sixty of us, thirty sat down—including me. *Gut* punch.

The first thing we learned at BOG was that our companies needed to have core values. It was step one of the program that taught some of the best and brightest entrepreneurs in the world how to manage, grow, and eventually sell their high-growth companies for seven-, eight-, nine-, and even ten-figure exits. We had built Twin Capital Mortgage from a one-room startup to 150 employees in just three short years. Twin Capital Mortgage was the fortieth-fastest-growing privately held company in the United States between 2003 and 2006. We had experienced over 2,500 percent revenue growth. The company ranked number forty in the prestigious Inc. 500 in 2007. The growth of Twin Capital Mortgage was unprecedented.

Today, however, I was to learn a valuable lesson about how little I knew about growing a business. All sixty of the CEOs who were part of the peer-to-peer Core Value Workshop had been in the BOG program for two years. After having two years to roll out core values in our companies, half of us sat down. John and Ken were about to show us who truly had core values in their company.

Let's make something crystal clear: 50 percent of the people in this room did not know their own core values. The same core values they had created themselves, just as I had. The core values they had rolled out in their organization in year one of BOG, just as I had. The core values that were supposedly what their companies stood for.

The next thirty seconds blew my mind.

Ken was still talking; the questions were not done. "Please stay standing if your *employees* know your core values and can say them off the top of *their* head."

Out of the remaining thirty who were standing, fifteen sat down. Half of the remaining half.

Then John spoke to the group of fifteen who were still standing: "Please stay standing if your *customers* know your core values."

And the entire room sat down, except for John and Ken. They were the only two people in our entire class, one night before we graduated, who could truly say they had core values in their company that were alive and well. They, their employees, and their customers all knew their core values.

I was in shock. At that moment, I realized that even among some of the most celebrated, influential, and experienced entrepreneurs I knew, none of us truly had core-value-driven companies.

That's not to say that we did not *have* core values in our companies. We did, but they weren't explicit, and people didn't know them. I realized that if you don't know your core values off the top of your head, and if your team doesn't know your core values off the top of their heads, then you really don't have core values that are alive and well in your company.

What you have is a group of people showing up every day, potentially doing great work, but doing so in their own way. You have an organization with a mix of different people's core values. I say this because:

Companies do not have core values; people have core values.

I repeat:

Companies do not have core values; people have core values.

When we are not explicit, intentional, and successful at rolling out the core values in our organization, we are forced to settle for a mixed bag of core values that each individual in our company brings to the organization. We get what we get, and we don't have control over the outcome. This is called inconsistency. If we and our team do not know the company's core values, then it is likely that we are not living them explicitly and consistently in everything we do. The reality is people are just doing their work based on their own core values. If we have hired perfectly, then this works out. I prefer not to bet on perfection, as this is not a way to scale a business.

For starters, let's get really clear on what a core-value-driven organization looks like. I define a core-value-driven organization as an organization where the values are lived consistently, and where people know and act based on the organization's values. It is a place where people hold one another accountable to this common set of values above all else. We cannot rely solely on the hope that we have hired the right people. Even if we have, there is no core value accountability unless the organization has explicitly said what it stands for and then created an environment that consistently holds everyone accountable to this standard. This is called consistency. This is where you have everyone aligned, doing things the same way, with the same care and love as you, the owner, would. You can only have an organization like this if your core values are alive and well in your organization.

It was John's last question that really opened up my thinking to how far you can take this if you truly lead with your core values in your company. *Please stay standing if your customers know your core values.* Think about this. If your customers don't share your core values, are they truly loyal to your business and products?

Let's take this a step further. Imagine you own a company backed by donors or investors, like private equity or venture capital—or even angel investors. Do your investors know and share your core values? What happens if there is a misalignment of core values with your investors when the business has a real issue? Will your investors have your back? When the going gets tough and you really need your investors or your teams to support you, what are the chances they will be there for you? Think about what this might look like if there is solid alignment around your core values versus inconsistency and lack of alignment around your core values.

If you want to have a core-value-driven organization, you really need to see alignment across the board—from leadership, to the team, to the customers, to your investors. When you have this alignment, the organization is truly poised for exponential growth.

This book is all about the process, best practices, and systemization around the question: *how do you build a core-value-driven organization?*

One of my favorite exercises is to ask founders, CEOs, and owners of businesses if their organizations have core values. They generally give me the same answer. "Yes, of course we have core values in our company." I then ask, "Okay, well, can you tell me what they are?"

I usually get a combination of "Courage…Errrrr…Mmmmmm…Integrity…" Crickets. They rarely know them. I am not saying that they do not run their business based on a set of core values that they themselves believe in. That is not the point of this book. Everyone goes through their day and makes decisions based on some set of values that they believe in. However, when you are running a business and those core values are not explicit, then they are not institutionalized in the company. When they are not institutionalized, then you get what you get.

Most people who start their companies do not see this until it is too late. I will give you the example of when I started Twin Capital Mortgage. When I started Twin Capital, it was me, my assistant, Jasmine, and our telemarketer, Al. We had one office that was about two hundred square feet. I got to come to that space every day and sprinkle my core values all over Jasmine and Al. It was magical. It felt like a small family. Does this sound familiar to you? Then we did what most great small businesses do: we started to grow. We hired another assistant, named Dane. Now it was Dane, Jasmine, Al, and I all working hard together. I did what I had always done, which was sprinkle my core values all over everyone. We all worked hard, and it felt like a family with shared values striving for a great outcome. I convinced my twin brother, Mike, to join the company as my business partner, and we got a second office in our building to support our growth. We also hired another assistant, named Angela, to help Jasmine with the administrative side of the business. Angela and Jasmine moved into the new office next door that shared a wall with the office Dane, Mike, Al, and I were in.

This is where I noticed a difference start to occur. There were two different cultures in the offices. In my office, it felt a lot more like the original culture that I described. The second office felt different. Not to say that it was bad in the second office—just different. Then we added another assistant to Jasmine and Angela's office, named Dani. There were two distinct cultures emerging in the two offices. Why wouldn't there be? The leaders in each room were different. The next thing we knew, we outgrew the space and moved into a much bigger office. This new office had three spaces, and each of these felt different when you walked into the room. It was one company, but the culture of each office exemplified the leaders of that office. Three offices turned into four, which turned into six, which turned into eight. Before I knew it, we had dozens of different cultures filled with a multitude of different core values. It all depended on which group you were talking to. This is what happens in most organizations. The core values and culture get diluted simply by the separation of a wall. Am I describing your organization right now?

As I noticed this dilution of the core values and culture occur at Twin Capital, I desperately tried to create some semblance of consistency. We had what are called "growing pains," which is really another way of describing friction throughout the organization. I had to bounce around from each room in the office daily to try to sprinkle my core values over different teams. It was marginally effective at best. It just depended on the manager who managed each specific office. If they were aligned with my core values, their office seemed to be more aligned with my expectations. If they were less aligned with my core values, the tone of that specific office seemed less aligned with my expectations. I was doing what most people do when they build an organization: trying my best. I was quickly learning that building a business without an explicit set of core values to drive the decision-making was not working well. I did not have a common set of core values that was alive and well in my organization, and I was paying the price.

Before I knew it, we had sixty employees in those eight offices, and we had bombs blowing up all over the business. My nickname for myself was "the firefighter." At this point, I had three departments: Loan Sales, Loan Processing, and Telemarketing. I would spend thirty days in Loan Sales and lower the temperature of the fire in that department. I would then need to go to Loan Processing to put out the fires in that department for thirty days, and then I would end up in Telemarketing to douse the fires there. Then back to Loan Sales...and on and on. It was frustrating beyond belief. I was exhausted. I was a twenty-seven-year-old CEO with a company that was constantly on fire and growing like crazy. The real issue was that I had created a business that I could not scale. We did not have consistency. There was no deliberate, known, measured, and managed set of core values that everyone abided by. Our policy and procedures—or lack thereof—did not create common and consistent outcomes. It all depended on how the staff was feeling that day.

What I am describing may sound familiar if you have managed a rapidly growing company. It could be inconsistencies within a department, from one location to another, or from one side of the building to the next, or inconsistencies based on the manager. All this boils down to an inconsistent experience for those inside and outside the organization.

Companies not grounded in a common set of core values are fragmented, and they are not set up to grow and scale. Core values, when implemented properly, become the language of the organization. Companies without consistent core values do not have a common language in their organization from which to scale. Basically, you have a group of people speaking their own languages when it comes to the work that is being done in the organization. What one person sees as hard work, responsibility, and being a team player, another may see as laziness, not taking ownership, and selfishness. When I approached Brian at our compliance desk, he and I were speaking two completely different languages. There was an inconsistency between our words and beliefs as they pertained to how we did our job, how we treated our customers, and what we wanted to contribute to make our company a great business. We were not speaking the same language as it pertained to Twin Capital Mortgage.

This book will teach you that anyone can have a business or organization that bleeds its core values day in and day out. It's there for the taking. Core values are the foundation of the business. Just as the foundation of a skyscraper must be strong, run deep into the ground, and be ready to hold up a large building, the core values of a business must be built strong in an organization to support the building of a great business. Consistency is paramount if we want to have a business that can grow and have an impact. This starts with creating a company that is centered around a common set of values that are scalable, sticky, and thriving in your organization regardless of location, manager, office, or department.

CONCLUSION

This book will show you how you can build the business of your dreams. I will leave you with this. When I sat down at BOG, I realized something that I hold with me to this day: if you, your team, and/or your investors don't know the core values of your company off the top of their heads, then you don't have a common set of core values. I did not have a common set of core values in my company on that day at MIT, and I needed to rebuild them for success.

CHAPTER 2

YOU DON'T KNOW HOW TO BUILD CORE VALUES

As my twin brother Mike likes to say, "Don't confuse effort with results."

I remember the moment I wrote down my core values and rolled them out to the company. There were six core values, with a total of seventy-six words. I laminated and hung them up all over our seventeen-thousand-square-foot office. I then created smaller versions for everyone to hang up in their cubicles and offices. I even created wallet-sized versions that we called "core value cards" for people to carry with them everywhere that they went. Life was good—we were now a core value company!

I then held a company-wide conference call so that all 150 of our employees could be formally introduced to the core values I had created. It was going to be magnificent. I had planned to get the team all on a call and to read them the core values. My goal was to explain to them that this is exactly what we at Twin Capital stood for, and that they were all expected to hold each other and the company accountable to these new and important core values. I was pumped, to say the least. I had the conference call and I introduced the core values to the entire company.

I started by explaining to the team the importance of core values. We were a core-value-driven organization. This is what we stood for as a company. I explained that it was important that we all lived these core values. I am sure many of you can relate to what I am talking about right now; this is a very common way to roll out core values. (For what it's worth, this is the worst way to roll out your core values. It is better than not having core values at all, but not effective if you are truly trying to build a core-value-driven organization. Not to worry, though—I will show you the right way later in the book. Promise.)

I was in the middle of reading the core values to the team (I had probably gotten through three or four of the six core values at this point) when one of our salespeople, who had accidentally not muted her phone, muttered, for the entire company to hear, "This is complete bullshit."

Looking back, I think this is hilarious. Not so much at the time.

My response was classic. I said, "Who said that? Who said that!?" I was so upset. I couldn't believe the disrespect. Someone was challenging our core values at *rollout*. But those words said it all: "This is such bullshit." And she was right. It was bullshit. I had done what my brother had warned against: confused effort with results. There were a lot of inconsistencies in the business at that point; it had issues. And so I had written an ambitious vision of what I wanted the company to look like, and, in my youthful exuberance, I had assumed our team felt the same way. I did not have their buy-in; I was shoving my core values down their throats. It was, as she had said, "complete bullshit."

Fast-forward to two years later. I was sitting in a diner in Cambridge, Massachusetts, reflecting on the happenings of Ken and John's peer-to-peer workshop (which I discussed in the last chapter). I should have been happy at that moment. I had just graduated from BOG and I had spent the last two years of my life transforming my company with everything I had learned from some of the best professors, speakers, and CEOs in the business world. But I was sitting in this diner, disappointed in myself. I had sat down during the workshop and I was haunted by this fact. What troubled me even more was that I was not the only person who'd sat down. Half of my classmates also sat down—all because of the simple question of whether we knew our core values. Indeed, this group of fifty-eight extremely accomplished CEOs had *all* sat down by the end of the exercise.

I was both intrigued and shocked by what I had witnessed. Here were some of the finest leaders I knew in the entire world, change-makers in industries from every continent. We were all taught the same things in BOG. We were all taught the best practices for building a great company. We were taught that our companies needed to have core values, and we were taught this on the first day of BOG. We designed and wrote them ourselves. They were our beliefs. We owned these values. They were our creations. We had then rolled them out into our companies. There could be no excuse regarding buy-in from the top of the organization. Yet here we were, two years later, at year three of BOG, standing amongst our peers and believing that we had core values in our businesses—yet we all sat down.

As I sat in the diner, I contemplated what had happened. Why did I not remember my core values? The answer was obvious. They were not easy to remember. Don't believe me? Here they are:

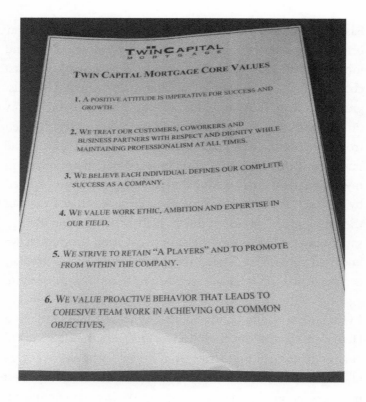

Six core values. Seventy-six words. They were long, generic, and not built for use. *Of course* I did not know my core values. The reality was that I had designed them very poorly. They were not bad core values from the standpoint of my intentions. These were great core values based on what they stood for and what they meant to me as the founder and CEO. I wanted great things for my company.

Let's take a look at what I created:

1. **A positive attitude is imperative for success and growth.**
   What this means: Positive attitudes are important for success
   in both business and life. Core value number one was all
   about positivity. This seems like a reasonable thing to want
   to have in your business.

2. **We treat our customers, coworkers, and business partners
   with respect and dignity, while maintaining professionalism at all times.** What this means: Don't be a jerk to
   everyone who works with you. I can get behind that. This is
   probably something we can all agree is important to a business if you want a high-performing organization. Respect,
   dignity, and professionalism—check!

3. **We believe each individual defines our complete success
   as a company.** What this means: Everyone's contribution to
   the win matters. Working together as a team is very important. Teamwork—check!

4. **We value work ethic, ambition, and expertise in our field.**
   What this means: We want our people to work hard and
   know their stuff. I can support this idea in any business
   that wants to have a strong team. Hard work and expertise—check!

5. **We strive to retain "A players"** and **promote from within
   the company.** What this means: We want the best people to
   work with us. We want to reward them. This is more of an
   HR policy, but not a terrible thing to shoot for. Top-talent
   core value—check!

6. **We value proactive behavior that leads to cohesive teamwork in achieving our common objectives.** What this
   means: Proactivity! More teamwork! I like all these things.

Do I need to nudge you awake after reading my core values from 2006?

I deserved to sit down that day. First of all, how did I expect anyone to remember any of this information? Second, these core values were completely generic. Seventy-six boring and generic words to describe six different core values in my business created exactly what I did not want: a set of core values built to fail. They were not built to be remembered by me or anyone, for that matter. I went back in time and thought about my intention when I had written these core values two years earlier. I had done a decent job of writing out the things I believed were most important to the business at that time. Clearly, these were great things to have in any company, and I was explicit and descriptive. But they were not memorable. A for effort, F for execution. As the salesperson said at my core value rollout: complete bullshit.

It's no surprise, then, that I sat down when asked if I remembered my core values, and fifty-seven other amazing, caring, core-value-driven CEOs sat down with me. We missed the boat on one of the most important parts of having a core-value-driven organization: the core values need to be memorable. If you can't remember them, then how can you expect them to be used in your company? My core values were relatable, but they were not well designed, and I did a poor job of making them come to life in the organization.

At the diner, I asked myself the following questions: *What do I really want my company to be? What type of business do I want to be a part of? What are the most important things I want Twin Capital to be known for? What makes Twin Capital, Twin Capital?* I started thinking back to the day I started the business, when I opened the doors for the first time. What was I looking to create at that moment? What made this company a place that got people excited to come to work? When I was hiring my first team members, what was I looking for in them? I realized that it was a reflection of who I was trying to be in the world. I believe that the best leaders and organizations do this. They try to create something that embodies their best attributes and aspirations.

I started thinking about what my staff complained about when things began going sideways in the company, when we started having "growing pains." What stood out to me the most was the nostalgia of "when it felt like a family." This may sound familiar; it happens all too often when companies grow quickly. It felt like a family, and now it does not. Or it felt like a family, and now it feels corporate. I think what people are trying to say is that, when it felt like a family, it felt like a place of shared values. We had begun the process of replacing a company with shared core values with one that was riddled with corporate infrastructure because we wanted consistency in the business. I see companies do this all the time. They lead with standard operating procedures, and policy and procedures, and not with core values. Why couldn't I have both? Why couldn't I have a company that felt like a family but was growing, scaling, and becoming professional? That is what I really wanted to build. I just didn't know how.

It was during this moment of contemplation that I had a glorious aha moment. It struck me that, in the exercise from the previous day, the only two people standing at the end of the exercise were Ken and John from Nurse Next Door. What happened next was my first step to righting the wrongs of the previous two years. I had been introduced to a concept known as R and D by a very influential person who shall remain nameless. He said, "When you see someone doing something well in their business that you wish you had in your business, just R and D it." Research and development? No—rip off and duplicate! Genius. I decided to R and D what Ken and John had done at their company, Nurse Next Door. I went to their website on my iPhone and looked up their core values.

Nurse Next Door's core values:

Admire People

Our clients aren't just case files. They're real people.

WOW Customer Experience

"Good" just won't do. We don't rest until we've exceeded expectations.

Find a Better Way

We try new things and grow through innovation.

Passionate About Making a Difference

We look for people who genuinely care about what they're doing.

I pulled up the following four core values, and I noticed something right away. First off, there were only four core values. Second, they were simple. Last, they stood for very big and important themes. It then hit me like a lightning bolt. But of course! The reason Ken and John stayed standing was so obvious: they only had four core values, they were simple, and they were what Nurse Next Door stood for. They were memorable and meaningful! My next steps were obvious. I was going to do what Nurse Next Door did—I was going to simplify my non-simplistic, boring, forgettable core values.

SIMPLIFYING MY CORE VALUES

I asked myself the following questions: *What do we want to be known for? What is most important to us at Twin Capital?* These were very easy questions for me to answer. I knew that we were a hardworking organization. We had an intense work ethic, and we had built the company with that expectation in mind. Having a strong work ethic was extremely important to us. The second thing that was important to us was having balance and integrity. It was important to us that people do the right thing. We believed in karma. You must remember this was 2008 and we were a mortgage lender. The mortgage industry had just blown up the world economy for making toxic loans—basically, not doing the right thing. We had just lived through a meltdown in our industry. We knew that doing the right thing was paramount to our future success. This was table stakes for us and still is.

The third thing that was important to us was having innovative thinkers in our company. We were a creative company and very entrepreneurial. We wanted people with an innovative mindset.

Finally, we were all about impressing our clients and impressing ourselves. This meant we were looking for people who wanted to show up to work to do a great job while striving to impress their customers and their coworkers. I really think that team members and customers are one and the same (internal and external clients). People who wanted to make this type of impression were a must for us!

Within minutes, I came up with the following core values:

- Do Work!
- Live Zen
- Break the Box
- Wow Everyone

It was simple. Do Work! meant exactly what it sounded like: work hard. Live Zen was about doing the right thing, having balance in our thinking, and having integrity. Break the Box was about being creative and innovative as an organization and in our approach. Wow Everyone was about trying to impress those around us, whether internal or external customers, with the way we work. This was about delivering amazing service inside and outside the organization.

Those were the four most important values that we wanted to be known for at Twin Capital. Hard work. Balance and integrity. Innovative creative thinking. Amazing service and making an impression. These were the areas that broke our hearts when we saw them missing in our company. I knew they had to be our focus for us to truly represent who we were to the world. There was no question about this in my mind.

When I was sixteen years old, my father gave me some sage advice that I have carried with me to this day. He told me: "Baba (it means son in Farsi), never listen to anyone who is not more successful than you are." The inverse of this is that if you want to do something better, look to someone who has done it better than you. I took that sage advice to heart that day in year three of BOG. Two CEOs stood before a group of peers, and they had done something better than anyone of us had. In their company, they had successfully rolled out core values that they and their team could remember. If I wanted my team and myself to remember our core values, they had to be easy to remember. It was as simple as that. I knew it was a start to my journey of truly building a core-value-driven organization.

I believe that most organizations get this wrong. They make their core values too complicated to remember. There are several factors to making the core values user-friendly that I will cover in this book. But the first lesson is to make them easy to remember. Making the core values user-friendly is an essential part of the discovery and design process.

Please let me make something crystal clear: **this is a discovery and design process**. I firmly believe that this is a mistake that most organizations fall into. They do not treat this as a discovery and design process. They build their house without a well thought out blueprint and then they are surprised when the windows are crooked. When we reframe core values in this way, we start to think about their use in our organization in an entirely new way.

CONCLUSION

When I first built my core values, I made the cardinal mistake of not being thoughtful about how they would be used in my organization. I created them without being thoughtful about the end user. This is the wrong approach. They were simply an item to check off the to-do list. For core values to become the language of the organization, they need to be set up for success. This first starts by designing them for mass adoption and use in the organization. We will now explore the different components necessary for the proper discovery and design of core values.

CHAPTER 3

WHAT CORE VALUES NEED TO BE TO WORK

Over the last twenty years of my experience as a CEO and entrepreneur, I have seen core values impact organizations in ways you would not imagine. This chapter will explore the four most critical elements that core values need in order to create consistent, impactful results in any organization:

1. Who Should Be Part of the Core Value Discovery and Design Process
2. Core Values Do Not Need to Be Nice
3. Invisible Scale
4. Trusting Your Core Values

1. WHO SHOULD BE PART OF THE CORE VALUE DISCOVERY AND DESIGN PROCESS

I am often asked by CEOs and founders whether their team should be involved with the creation of the core values in the organization. First, we should address the word "creation" versus "discovery." In Verne Harnish's book Scaling Up, Harnish best sums up what a company is when he states the following, "…your company is a living breathing organism with a distinct personality. It expresses that personality through its Values." Harnish goes on to state, "Discerning the Core Values is a DISCOVERY process, not the creation of a wish list of nice-to-haves."[1] The goal of the discovery process is to identify what the company culture is at its core and to establish a starting set of values from which to work from. Once the starting values are identified through the discovery process, the senior leadership will need to spend time and energy designing these values into the finished core values that the company will use in everything that it does.

I feel strongly that the people who should be involved in the discovery and design of the core values are the senior leaders of the organization who have a strong sense of what core values stand out within the organization and what the company truly is at its core.

A few years ago, I saw a Twitter post from *Inc.* magazine quoting the CEO of Tatcha. In the post she stated the following:

"The team came up with what the company values are. They weren't the ones I created and dictated." —Victoria Tsai, Founder, Tatcha

---

1   Verne Harnish, Scaling Up: How a Few Companies Make It… and Why the Rest Don't (Gazelles Inc.: 2014), 94-96.

I responded to this post:

"No offense but when the team is gone and you are stuck with their values you may second guess this method."
—Darius, Tweet to Victoria Tsai, November 16, 2015

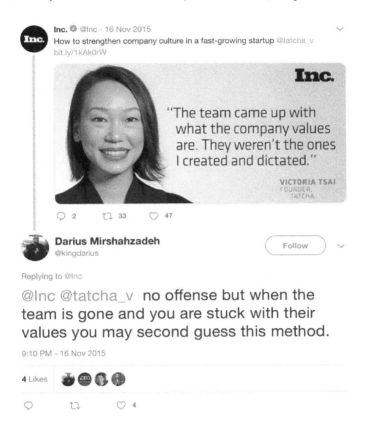

According to the Bureau of Labor Statistics, as of November 1, 2018, the median number of years that wage and **salary workers** have worked for their current employer is currently 4.6 years. However, this longevity varies by age and occupation.

The median tenure for **workers** age twenty-five to thirty-four is **3.2 years.**[2]

Table 1. Median years of tenure with current employer for employed wage and salary workers by age and sex, selected years, 2008-2018

AGE AND SEX	JAN 2008	JAN 2010	JAN 2012	JAN 2014	JAN 2016	JAN 2018
TOTAL						
16 years and over	4.1	4.4	4.6	4.6	4.2	4.2
16 to 17 years	0.7	0.7	0.7	0.7	0.6	0.6
18 to 19 years	0.8	1.0	0.8	0.8	0.8	0.8
20 to 24 years	1.3	1.5	1.3	1.3	1.3	1.2
25 years and over	5.1	5.2	5.4	5.5	5.1	5.0
25 to 34 years	2.7	3.1	3.2	3.0	2.8	2.8
35 to 44 years	4.9	5.1	5.3	5.2	4.9	4.9
45 to 54 years	7.6	7.8	7.8	7.9	7.9	7.6
55 to 64 years	9.9	10.0	10.3	10.4	10.1	10.1
65 years and over	10.2	9.9	10.3	10.3	10.3	10.2
MEN						
16 years and over	4.2	4.6	4.7	4.7	4.3	4.3
16 to 17 years	0.7	0.7	0.6	0.7	0.6	0.5
18 to 19 years	0.8	1.0	0.8	0.9	0.8	0.8
20 to 24 years	1.4	1.6	1.4	1.4	1.3	1.3
25 years and over	5.2	5.3	5.5	5.5	5.2	5.1
25 to 34 years	2.8	3.2	3.2	3.1	2.9	2.9
35 to 44 years	5.2	5.3	5.4	5.4	5.0	5.0
45 to 54 years	8.2	8.5	8.5	8.2	8.4	8.1
55 to 64 years	10.1	10.4	10.7	10.7	10.2	10.2
65 years and over	10.4	9.7	10.2	10.0	10.2	10.2
WOMEN						
16 years and over	3.9	4.2	4.6	4.5	4.0	4.0
16 to 17 years	0.6	0.7	0.7	0.7	0.6	0.7
18 to 19 years	0.8	1.0	0.8	0.8	0.8	0.8
20 to 24 years	1.3	1.5	1.3	1.3	1.2	1.2
25 years and over	4.9	5.1	5.4	5.4	5.0	4.9
25 to 34 years	2.6	3.0	3.1	2.9	2.6	2.7
35 to 44 years	4.7	4.9	5.2	5.1	4.8	4.7
45 to 54 years	7.0	7.1	7.3	7.6	7.5	7.1
55 to 64 years	9.8	9.7	10.0	10.2	10.0	10.1
65 years and over	9.9	10.1	10.5	10.5	10.4	10.1

NOTE: Updated population controls are introduced annually with the release of January data.

---

2 Bureau of Labor Statistics, "Employee Tenure in 2018," (news release, Washington, 2018).

The problem with allowing your team to come up with the core values is simple. Depending on the age of your team, there is a very high likeliness that the team who creates those values will not be there to live them with you. This is a major problem for the senior leadership who are left with someone else's core values defining the culture of the company.

Core values need to be authentic to the soul of the organization. It is especially important that senior leadership lead by example. Their behavior and actions must be fully aligned with the core values of the company. Senior leadership cannot break the core values. A core value breach at this level completely undermines the validity of the values in the organization. The only way to guarantee a breach never happens is by making sure that the values are discovered and designed by the senior leadership who truly know the personality of the organization.

In 2018, I was introduced to an amazing concept around what determines *results* in our lives. I was working with performance coach Dr. David Zelman of the Transitions Institute when he introduced me to a very powerful equation. I had an amazing aha moment a couple months after our coaching. I realized how his equation connected with the core value work I have been doing for all these years. The idea is basic:

Our core values drive our decisions. Our decisions drive our actions. Our actions drive our results.

CORE VALUES = DECISIONS = ACTIONS = RESULTS

Core values need to represent exactly what the business will stand for in all situations where a decision is made. When designed and implemented properly, core values become the ultimate decision-making engine for an organization. Core values need to effectively represent the expectations of the company in all scenarios that the business may encounter. This is why it is so important that the core values are authentic to the organization.

Based on this idea, let's take a look at the Twitter comment I made to Victoria Tsai in 2015. Victoria Tsai thought it was a good idea to allow her team to create the core values for the company, Tatcha. It was important to her that she did not "create or dictate" what the core values were to her team.

On the surface, I get what she is trying to do. People buy into things when it is their idea—especially if it represents *their* core values. It makes complete sense why someone might think that this is a best practice for the creation of core values. The problem lies in a couple of areas. First, the organization and senior leadership need to have complete alignment around the values. If the senior leadership is not involved in the discovery and design of the core values, then there is no guarantee of this alignment. If the team chooses values that do not align to what the organization truly is at its core, you have a huge problem. You have a much higher likeliness of inconsistencies in what happens in the company. This is because there is now a misalignment around core values that affects decision-making as illustrated in the equation above. Any potential issue that allows inconsistency needs to be eliminated from an organization if it wants to scale and succeed.

Second, the integrity of the leadership is at risk if there is a possible misalignment with the core values that the team creates. I say the following with full conviction: the day the leadership of the organization does not live the core values consistently and/or breaks the core values in a meaningful way is the day you have put a bullet in the head of your company core values. This undermines the culture, leadership, and alignment of the company with everyone who **does** believe in the stated values from that point forward. We often see this in organizations where they have created core values and promoted them, but they are meaningless because the team sees the leadership not living the core values consistently. The risk is far too high to ever consider doing this in a company. This is a culture killer.

Last, since we can see that the average life of an employee in your company is going to be less than five years, having them create the core values or have any real influence in the core value discovery and design process is an issue. (There are, however, wonderful ways to get their buy-in that I will explore in later chapters.) In my experience, having the team dictate the core values can really jeopardize the act of bringing those values to life and keeping them alive in your organization.

2. CORE VALUES DO NOT NEED TO BE NICE

Core values, when they are alive and well in an organization, are an amazing filtration tool that self-selects people who believe what the company believes. This is why it is so important that core values be authentic to the organization at its core. I say the next statement with complete sincerity: *core values do not need to be nice*. I often find that when I start talking about core values in business, there are two different mindsets. One gets it. Core values are the fabric of our society—to have them in a business makes sense, as people have core values in their personal lives, families, community organizations, political parties, religions, and many other important parts of their lives. The other cohort looks at me like I am talking about going on a silent meditation retreat with my accounting team. It just does not click. I believe the latter sees this type of stuff as "new age" and "fluff." In some organizations, this probably is fluff.

If we say, "Core values do not need to be nice," these non-believers will often see the light. Many organizations try to make their core values all-inclusive, safe, and very vanilla. The core values are not authentic to what they truly believe. This is playing politics with yourself and your team. I am not suggesting that choosing authenticity is easy, but it is imperative when we are trying to create a high-performing core-value-driven organization. When we are authentic, we get to show everyone exactly what we are. This has the possibility of alienating some people. Great! Those people will never be your raving fan base. I would rather find a smaller group of raving fans than a larger group of apathetic people who show up for a paycheck. *Core values do not need to be nice.*

If you are a company filled with sarcastic, offensive, trash-talking workaholics, then your core values should align to people who will like being in this type of environment.

For instance, I know a CEO named Mark. Mark runs a management consulting company called Hilltop Consulting. Hilltop is filled with folks who graduated from the best MBA programs in the United States.

The culture of Hilltop looks like this: The team works eighty hours a week, never take lunch breaks, and are workaholics. Hilltop is an aggressive environment where people compete against each other to be the best, day in and day out. The team at Hilltop challenge the status quo and debate each other's thoughts and ideas. Curiosity, courage, and assertiveness are all behaviors that are celebrated at Hilltop, especially when it comes to making Hilltop a better company. Hilltop is filled with soldiers who will come to work ready to kill the competition. Hilltop is a company where the team bleeds the company colors. Hilltop aspires to become a monster of a business. Winning is everything at Hilltop.

This is likely not a company that many people will enjoy working at if they are not aggressive, competitive, and at the stage in their life where they are okay working seventy to one hundred hours per week. The team at Hilltop has a couple of options when building their core values. They can play it safe and do what many companies do. They can go the vanilla route, and their core values will look something like this:

- Integrity
- Customer First
- Balance
- Family
- Fun

These five terms probably look like a generic set of core values that we often see in companies. The problem with these core values is that they sound **nothing** like the company I described above. If I applied to work at Hilltop and got the job, I would have no idea what I was really walking into. This is a massive failure for Hilltop and for the new hire. These passive, vanilla core values have not done their job in creating alignment in the organization. They have, however, bred mistrust and made a mockery of the core values. These are what I call "words on paper." They are not authentic to the actual beliefs of the company, and they really serve no purpose in the organization except to fill up a little space on a piece of paper that HR hands to the new employee on their first day.

If Hilltop had gone through a true discovery process and then designed authentic, non-vanilla core values in their organization, they might look more like this:

- Passion
- Steel Sharpens Steel
- All In
- Warrior Culture
- Tough Love

It is highly likely that these core values will turn some people off. That is a huge *win* for Mark and his organization. This is called self-selection. You want the core values to stop the wrong people from ever joining the organization. Inversely, you want the *authentic* core values to become a magnet for people who believe what Hilltop believes. There is a community of people who will be turned on by Hilltop's hard-core approach. When they join the company, they will feel connected to Hilltop's warrior culture. They will not get offended when people are battling and testing each other internally. They have likely been doing this their entire lives in sports, school, and the competitive groups that they were in. They will have now found a home at Hilltop. This is what I call organizational alignment, and it is probably the most powerful element a winning organization can have. This all starts with having authentic core values.

A great example of this are the original core values that Travis Kalanick and his team built at Uber. Many people would say that it was a toxic culture to a certain degree—one that had questionable integrity and a winning-at-all-cost ethos. Travis and his team were not quiet about this.

Although I have a lot to say about the design of Uber's core values (it needs a lot of work), what these stated values say, and the degree to which they came to life, says a lot about the organization that was built under Travis until his departure.

Uber Core Values:[3]

1. Super-pumpedness
2. Always be hustlin'
3. Let builders build
4. Meritocracy and toe-stepping
5. Principled confrontation
6. Making bold bets
7. Celebrate cities
8. Make magic
9. Inside out
10. Optimistic leadership
11. Being yourself
12. Own don't rent
13. Champion's mindset
14. Obsession with the customer

Individually, many of these are great ideas that are not toxic to a culture. They may even work well depending on the leadership that is implementing them. But when you start to celebrate fierceness, confrontation, toe-stepping, and the like, you are walking a fine line. In the case of Uber, this led to some alleged less-than-good behavior and, in many cases, created a toxic culture when it got to a certain scale. On the one hand, this is a prime example of core values going sideways in an organization.

---

3   Mike Isaac, "Inside Uber's Aggressive, Unrestrained Workplace Culture," *New York Times*, February 22, 2017; Brad Stone, *The Upstarts: How Uber, Airbnb, and the Killer Companies of the New Silicon Valley Are Changing the World* (New York: Little, Brown, 2017); Oliver Staley, "Uber Has Replaced Travis Kalanick's Values With Eight New Cultural Norms," *Quartz*, November 8, 2017.

On the other hand, this aggressive set of values, celebration of pushing one another, and "fierceness" is likely what led Uber to become one of the most valuable companies in the world. It is easy to criticize Kalanick in retrospect. When the scandals surrounding their culture came to life in the media, I was not surprised. But this is also an example of an organization discovering and promoting their authentic core values to create something extraordinary. For that, I give credit to Kalanick and the team. They had authentic core values built into their organization, and the world is now forever changed.

The more authentic you can be with your core values, the greater an opportunity you are going to have to get the right people on the bus and have the wrong people self-select out. This is probably one of the most powerful discoveries I have made in my exploration of creating core-value-driven companies. Once this happens, you start to see the magic. This is where we start to experience the power of synergy in our organizations. There is a quote I love that sums this up perfectly:

"If there is no common set of values, there can be no vision of the future."

Having this level of alignment around a common set of core values—good, bad, or indifferent—creates a consistency in the organization. Your people know what to expect from each other, and they know what to expect from the leadership. That creates consistency from a customer standpoint as well.

Now that we understand what core values need to be—i.e., authentic to the personality of the company and reflective of your company's real character (not necessarily nice)—I want to explore what good core values can create: invisible scale.

3. INVISIBLE SCALE

What is invisible scale? I would explain it as this. If I can build a core-value-driven organization, then I have a company where the core values are alive and well: an organization where the values drive the decisions, which drive the actions, which then equals the results that we produce. When I have done this, I have created the most powerful invisible manager in the world. I have created a manager that sits at the desk of every team member, participating in every action and every outcome, and I have done this without hiring a single person to do it. Instead, I have the team micromanaging themselves according to a common set of beliefs. My core values have become my manager, and I have built one of the most powerful tools that an organization can possess. This tool is known as invisible scale. You cannot see it, but it is everywhere, and it can create amazing consistency in an organization. The power can be unprecedented when it comes to scaling a company.

What this looks like in real life is this: if I have a group of people that all believe the same things, then their behavior and their actions are going to be consistent. I don't need to look over their shoulder or double-check them. They're just going to naturally do the things that I, as a leader, would do if I were in their shoes. I don't have to train for that, because I am hiring based on core value alignment. When my team and I have those shared values, it is much easier to naturally have the same outcomes happen in the business. That's invisible scale.

This is not to say you throw out policy and procedure, proper onboarding, or training. Those are all very important elements of scale as well. It does, however, mean that there is a cultural efficiency that comes into play. My people will seemingly work better together because they have a common set of beliefs.

Going back to our example of Hilltop's warrior culture, let's say Hilltop hires Kelly from a nonprofit. Kelly came highly recommended from one of Mark's friends, had great references, and is very smart and outgoing. Kelly is a team player, but she values her work/life balance. Kelly takes one-hour lunches, needs her fifteen-minute breaks every four hours, and leaves at 5:00 p.m. on the dot every day. The rest of the team is aggressive, works through lunch, and stays late burning the midnight oil together. You can't tell me that this will not create problems in the organization. Even if Kelly's quality of work is fantastic, she will probably feel like an outsider who is not doing enough. Her coworkers will not respect her work ethic. This is an example of misalignment, which is the opposite of invisible scale. You may have infighting or emotions regarding inequality in the team—none of which has anything to do with the work that needs to get done.

However, if Hilltop has ten people on the team who share a similar ethos around the warrior culture, they are finishing each other's sentences and thoughts. Hilltop then has cultural efficiency, and invisible scale is created. The foundation of this is building a core-value-driven organization with authentic core values as the bedrock of the company. Using the example of Kelly working in Mark's organization, one of two things is likely to occur. Either Kelly will self-select herself out of the organization, or Mark will tolerate this inconsistency in the culture. If Mark is supporting Hilltop's warrior culture, Kelly will feel out of place, or Mark will look like a hypocrite to the rest of his team for creating a double standard in the organization. In my experience, when you have a cultural misfit, it will likely dilute the culture.

For the sake of argument, let's use another example at Hilltop. As a reminder, these are Hilltop's core values:

- Passion
- Steel Sharpens Steel
- All In
- Warrior Culture
- Tough Love

There are times that people who are not a good fit for our organizations make it through the hiring process. Let's say Hilltop has another employee, named Peter. Peter surfs the web when he is supposed to be working. He takes seven smoke breaks a day, is the least productive person on the team, and even watches movies at his desk when he is supposed to be working. The rest of Hilltop's team are a bunch of assassins, subscribing to the warrior culture I described above. What happens if Mark tolerates Peter's behavior? The number-one thing that is likely to happen is that the rest of the team will feel like the core values are not as true as they once were. This will lead to a dilution of the culture, which will lead to the team not being managed to the high standards that Hilltop claims to believe in. Peter is a core value misfit when it comes to the following core values:

- All In
- Warrior Culture
- Passion

If Mark does not live up to Hilltop's core value of Tough Love and manage Peter up or out of the organization, then he is undermining the company's core values. What tends to happen when action is not taken to uphold the core values is the most tragic thing we see in organizations. The core values become invalidated, and the team loses faith that they are a true representation of the organization. We then tend to see the team measure themselves against the lowest common denominator. In this case, the lowest common denominator's name is Peter. **The core values must be authentic from top to bottom in the organization.** Peter must be managed up or out of the company, or he will become the new standard of accepted performance in the group. Think of your organization. Do you have a Peter or Kelly? We all do from time to time. Some of you may have many Peters and Kellys in your companies. The question I ask is simple: *what standard are you measuring them against from a core value perspective?*

4. TRUSTING YOUR CORE VALUES

Sometimes following your core values is an easy decision. But life and people are not black and white. People generally have good qualities to them. People generally embody some of the core values you have in your company. However, alignment in a company is not part-time. Consistency requires organizations to look for core value and cultural alignment 100 percent of the time. They will always have work to do to get back to that standard when they fail. In the case of Peter not being a cultural fit, I do not believe that you fire him right away. I think we have an obligation to give those we employ an opportunity to live up to the core values and standards of the organization. The exception to this is a severe breach, like fraud, or lying, or cheating. But that is rare. Usually, the breaches lie in the gray area. In those instances, we need to coach and counsel and give the teammate an opportunity to right the wrong. When this does not happen in a timely manner, then we owe that individual, the team, and the company the opportunity to part ways. Trust me, you are doing everyone a favor, especially the person who is not a core value fit. There is likely a great home for them outside your organization. They deserve the opportunity to thrive in a place where they are culturally aligned. When you, as the leader, make the tough decision to part ways with those who are not aligned with your company core values, you are making a statement to those who remain that the core values are extremely important. Most importantly, you are validating the existence of the core values within the organization. When Hilltop says they only want people who embody the warrior culture and asks those who are not a fit to leave, the warrior culture is never more alive and well than at that moment. Mark has just paid into the till on his company's core values being true, alive, and unquestionable even when it means making a tough call. This is not to say that firing a teammate is no big deal. This is the ultimate responsibility of the leader and the organization. The core values must always come first if you truly want to have a core-value-driven organization.

Another tough example of this is when we have *top producers* who are cultural misfits. I have had this a few times in my organizations. It is probably one of the toughest decisions a company can make. I will use a great example to illustrate. Sandy owns a company called A-Team Insurance that has an outside sales team of thirty salespeople. The top producer at A-Team is Janson. Janson crushes it. At A-Team, Janson accounts for 20 percent of the sales out of a team of thirty salespeople. Janson is what I like to call a "sales animal." Janson eats, sleeps, and breathes closing deals and is one of the most competitive people I have ever met. Sandy has a problem, though: Janson is not only aggressive when it comes to closing deals; Janson is aggressive to the entire company as well. To Janson, the customer gets 100 percent of his love, even at the expense of Sandy's company and support team. Janson has made team members cry on multiple occasions with his hot-headed behavior and an aggressive approach. Janson loves to email in ALL CAPS, which everyone interprets as YELLING OVER EMAIL (and ALL CAPS *is* yelling in the world of email). Janson is painful to work with, and Sandy is constantly putting out fires from the internal messes he creates with his behavior. A-Teams' core values are as follows:

- Caring Culture
- Be a Leader
- Think Creatively
- Service First

Although Janson is an amazing near-term financial asset to the company, Janson does not live up to the following core values of A-Team:

- Caring Culture
- Be a Leader

Janson breaks these core values every day. Janson is all about Janson being number one. He is damn good at being number one too. But Janson is not a core value fit. Sandy has fantasized about firing Janson. But Janson is 20 percent of the revenue; if he left, A-Team would potentially lose 20 percent of their business overnight. In a business that has fixed expenses and mediocre profit margins, that could easily be the difference between profit and loss.

Have you ever had a Janson in your company? Most of us—if not all of us—have. The right thing to do is not always the easiest thing to do. It is easy to say just fire Janson. When you have the courage it takes to face the fear of loss at the expense of living up to the core values, then you will truly know if the core values are alive and well in your organization. Are you willing to sell your core values for a top producer? When you choose the top producer over the core values, you are selling your soul to the almighty dollar. Many people do this—*I* have done it, but I have always regretted it afterward. In hindsight, the tough choice has always been the right choice, and I paid one way or the other. I paid in the form of lost opportunities internally or externally, as those top producers tended to turn off other top producers from joining my company. I paid in the form of turnover from people who refused to work with the nightmare top producer. I paid in the form of hidden costs as well. Hidden costs are what happens when these hostile top producers create fear in my company—it leads to people hiding and not giving me 100 percent of their effort. I paid with my own time, having to clean up the mess that these hostile interactions created in the company. One way or the other, we always pay when there is a cultural misfit.

The biggest expense, however, is that A-Team's core values are invalidated by Janson's behavior, and this breeds mistrust and lack of alignment in the organization. This prevents invisible scale from existing. I will bet dollars to donuts that financially, this will cost the company in revenue numbers that pale in comparison to the 20 percent of revenue Janson is bringing in. Top producers will come and go, but core values create value that no one person can offer in any organization. There is no question in my mind that the tradeoff is never worth the value that the top producer might bring. Do you have the courage to hold your core values high when push comes to shove and you need to ask a top producer to be successful elsewhere? The Peters of the world are an easy decision to make; the Jansons, however, are where the rubber meets the road.

Whether it's a top producer in sales, an operations rock star, an all-star executive, or an administrative badass—if someone puts themselves ahead of the needs of the organization or simply does not share the same values, they have to go! That is the moment of truth when it comes to measuring the organization against its values. When a company is willing to give up someone who creates immediate and recognizable value for the betterment and sanctity of the values within the organization, this is when you know the core values are alive and well.

Well-designed core values that are alive and well in an organization will answer the question posed in any decision in the organization. My business partners and I today use our core values to answer the toughest questions. We do this all the time, but especially when it is a decision that we are having a tough time making. We will say what the problem is. We will then read our core values out loud to one another, take a moment, and then discuss what the core values say we need to do. I have yet to encounter one decision for which the core values did not give us the answer. I am talking about the toughest decisions a company can make, like selling a business or reduction-in-force types of decisions. All of the time, the core values have clearly told us what we need to do. Most of those times, my stomach turns because it is usually the decision I do not want to make, but this method has never failed me. I believe it is the most powerful tool we have in our company today. I attribute much of our success to being able to use our core values in this way.

Remember:

CORE VALUES = DECISIONS = ACTIONS = RESULTS

Are you willing to stand up for the core values in your company?

The results you yield will depend on this. The core values are a filter for all decision-making in a core-value-driven organization.

CONCLUSION

By having the senior-level leadership discover and design core values that are authentic to the company, we create an organization where invisible scale can become the oxygen in the air of the organization. Those who approach their core values with these elements in mind are positioned for massive scale and consistency from the top all the way throughout the entire organization. The next chapter will introduce the discovery and design process around building core values that last.

CHAPTER 4

BUILDING CORE VALUES THAT LAST

"I thought my dad's sense of design was pretty good," Steve Jobs told Walter Isaacson, "because he knew how to build anything. If we needed a cabinet, he would build it. When he built our fence, he gave me a hammer so I could work with him."

Fifty years after the fence was constructed, Jobs showed it to Isaacson—it was still standing. He recalled a lesson about making things of quality that he had learned from his father. Touching the boards of the inside of the fence, he said, "He loved doing things right. He even cared about the look of the parts you couldn't see."[4]

In an interview a few years later, after the Macintosh came out, Jobs again reiterated that lesson from his father. "When you're a carpenter making a beautiful chest of drawers, you're not going to use a piece of plywood on the back even though it faces the

---

4   Walter Isaacson, *Steve Jobs* (New York: Simon & Schuster, 2011), 6.

wall, and nobody will ever see it. You'll know it's there. So you're going to use a beautiful piece of wood in the back for you to sleep well at night. The aesthetic, the quality, has carried all the way through."[5]

In this chapter I will first be diving into three key ideas when it comes to using design thinking in the creation of our core values. We will then examine two companies and how their ability to live up to their core values has defined their products and customer experiences. And last, I will introduce the first step to designing our core values, known as our core value themes:

1. Design Thinking with Core Values
2. A Tale of Two Companies
3. Core Value Themes

1. DESIGN THINKING WITH CORE VALUES

The story above emphasizes the importance of design thinking and the quality and craftsmanship that should go into any design process. You might be asking yourself, "Why are we talking about this when we're talking about core values?" I think that's the biggest mistake people make when they design their core values. They are not thinking of the craftsmanship and the usability of the product itself (in this case, the product is the core values). I see this all too often. There appears to be little design in most company's core values. They are thought of as something you build, roll out, and then hope will come alive in your company. This is wishful thinking, especially at scale. If this book teaches you anything, it is this: if you were to treat your core values like a product that needs to be used

---

5   David Sheff, "Playboy Interview: Steve Jobs," *Playboy*, February 1, 1985, 14.

by an end user, then wouldn't you focus on designing a great product that is easy to use and well made? Wouldn't you make it a product that people are excited to share with those they know and respect and that they want these others to use as well? Wouldn't you make it elegant and user-friendly so that people in your company are more likely to adopt it as a tool that they are excited to use all the time? This all requires design thinking and intentionality around how the end user will use the product once it is given to them.

Steve Jobs is famous for his approach to integrating design thinking into everything that Apple did under his watch. Apple built one of the largest and most valuable companies in the world because of its intentionality around great design and because the company was fanatic about the user experience. It is no wonder that Jobs felt this way given how he was brought up. His father taught him to care about the craftsmanship of the wood in a cabinet that no one would ever see. It is this attention to detail and quality that creates something of lasting value. The next two chapters will take this ethos around design, craftsmanship, and intentionality and apply it to how we design the core values in our organizations.

Jobs's obsession with design in his products created some of the most used and iconic products the world has ever seen. A September 2012 article published by *Smithsonian Magazine* discussed Jobs's approach to design when it came to the iPod, which arguably changed the trajectory of Apple and product design:

> Jobs' belief in the power of simplicity as a design precept reached its pinnacle with the three consumer device triumphs he produced beginning in 2001: the iPod, iPhone and iPad. He immersed

himself daily in the design of the original iPod and its interface. His main demand was "Simplify!" He would go over each screen and apply a rigid test: if he wanted a song or a function, he should be able to get there in three clicks. And the click should be intuitive. If he couldn't figure out how to navigate to something, or if it took more than three clicks, he would be brutal.[6]

This same thinking should be applied to the core values of an organization. How they are designed will define how they are used in an organization. The design will also have a material impact on the relevance of the core values and their usefulness in the long run. Going back to the lessons Jobs learned from his father and then later implemented in the design of the iPod, iPhone, and iPad, we see that great design withstands the test of time. We see this when a piece of furniture is well built; we see this in the fence described at the beginning of this chapter. Your core values deserve the same care, intentionality, and quality of design if they are also to be properly adopted in your organization.

2. A TALE OF TWO COMPANIES

I often tell people that your culture and core values define the products and services that your company produces. I touched on this a bit in the last chapter with our equation:

CORE VALUES = DECISIONS = ACTIONS = RESULTS

I view the products and services of an organization as the *results* that an organization produces. This is especially noticeable in

---

6   Walter Isaacson, "How Steve Jobs' Love of Simplicity Fueled A Design Revolution," *Smithsonian Magazine*, September 2012, https://www.smithsonianmag.com/arts-culture/how-steve-jobs-love-of-simplicity-fueled-a-design-revolution-23868877/.

a service-based organization, where the product is the service itself. But product-based companies are not immune to this dynamic, as there is generally some level of customer service required. This makes the intentionality and the adoption of the core values more important than ever, as it defines how our customers will interact with our brands and products.

An example of this would be an interaction I had with two companies not too long ago. A couple of years ago, I bought a wireless Bluetooth speaker for my house from Best Buy. I was having some technical issues getting it to work and decided to call Best Buy to get some help. What transpired next was complete chaos. I called in and went through their *painful* phone tree. Finally, I got someone on the phone after what seemed like an eternity. This individual sounded nothing short of apathetic and disinterested in my issue. About thirty seconds in, the call got disconnected. I blew a gasket. I then proceeded to go back into customer-service purgatory and live through the same experience again. The next customer-service rep sounded like a zombie. The Best Buy customer-service team sounded like they hated their jobs. Two minutes into the second call, guess what happened? You probably guessed correctly—I got disconnected again. I nearly lost my mind. All I kept thinking was: *How can you have a company that gives such low regard to the customer experience?* I called a third time. This time, I was tired. I was beaten down. I was disgusted. In my mind, I swore to never give this company a dollar of my money again. I slogged through the pain of their phone tree for the third time. After a few minutes, I pounded out and got the Geek Squad on the phone. Before I began, I asked for the person's direct number and gave them mine. I then asked to speak to a supervisor and, after a few minutes of grumbling and complaining about what transpired, I booked the Geek Squad. This entire process lasted nearly forty-five minutes and Best Buy had successfully made me hate their company. They had created a loyal detractor. A detractor is someone who talks trash about a business every chance they get. I could not believe how bad a customer experience I had had. I told my business partner that we should "short the Best Buy stock" (this is what you do when you think a company is going downhill and you want to make money on the stock price going down).

For fun, I pulled up Best Buy's core values to test these against my experience with them and their zombie customer-service team:

Best Buy's core values are:[7]

- Unleash the power of our people
- Learn from challenge and change
- Show respect, humility, and integrity
- Have fun while being the best

My experience that day told me that Best Buy had not done a good job of bringing their core values to life. This is a great example of "words on paper." Best Buy's written core values were nowhere to be found based on my experience that day.

Your core values are your product. If they are alive and well, your products and services will reflect this. If not, the company will get inconsistency and have an inferior product compared to competitors who have succeeded in defining and bringing their core values to life. If Best Buy had done a great job of bringing their values to life that day, I, as the customer, would have had a completely different experience.

---

7   Best Buy, "Culture," http://www.bestbuy-jobs.com/culture/.

A few days later, I had an issue pop up with my iPhone. I had dropped my iPhone into the pool and needed to figure out how to get a new phone. I called up Apple to speak with AppleCare about dealing with my now sponge of an iPhone. At the back of my mind, I was thinking of my experience with Best Buy a few days earlier. My experience with Apple could not have been more different. The phone tree was interactive, and there was obviously a lot of thought given to the customer experience. I quickly made my way to the AppleCare representative. It took no more than one to two minutes before someone was helping me. The gentleman I was speaking to was extremely friendly. I will never forget the first two things he said to me. First and foremost, he asked me for my phone number; in the event that we got disconnected, he would call me back. Second, he referenced the last issue I had called in on to make sure the issue had not persisted and was resolved.

I remember thinking about the difference between the two experiences with these consumer-electronics giants. It was night and day. On one side of the fence, you had a painful, stereotypically bad customer-service call center experience with Best Buy. The Best Buy team member was trudging through their day and did not care about me as a customer. I was a chore. Best Buy was not thoughtful about my experience with their phone tree, about the energy of their team, or about being proactive to mitigate issues like us getting disconnected and me having to go back through the painful process of calling them. Best Buy did not appear to value their customers or their employees—at least, that was the feeling I was left with.

On the other hand, you have one of the most valuable, profitable companies in the world, and everything they were doing was the opposite of this. Not only do they have amazing products that are thoughtful and have great design, but they also take that same care into designing their customer service. They understand that your culture and values are your product in a service-based and product-based economy. Kudos to Steve Jobs for building that fifty-year fence that we call Apple. Bravo.

For comparison, here are Apple's core values (they need to do some work on their design, but clearly, they have built a culture that supports these being true at Apple).

- We believe that we're on the face of the Earth to make great products.
- We believe in the simple, not the complex.
- We believe that we need to own and control the primary technologies behind the products we make.
- We participate only in markets where we can make a significant contribution.
- We believe in saying no to thousands of projects so that we can really focus on the few that are truly important and meaningful to us.
- We believe in deep collaboration and cross-pollination of our groups, which allow us to innovate in a way that others cannot.
- We don't settle for anything less than excellence in every group in the company, and we have the self-honesty to admit when we're wrong and the courage to change.[8]

Apple lived up to their core values that day! They had made their phone tree simple and user-friendly. They were proactive in their approach. Finally, they gave me excellent service. This is a tale of two companies. One with a great culture that

---

8   Apple, "Apple Earnings Call Transcript for Quarter Ending 12-27-08," January 21, 2009.

permeates into everything they do. Another with a lot of work to do, and core values and culture that are not aligned with what they say they are.

Are your product and culture aligned? Are you and your team making your customer experience consistent with what you say you are all about? Do your customers think you are living up to your core values? All too often, I find that there is a disconnect in what many companies say they are and what they actually are. Remember, your core values define the results of your organization. The coming chapters are all about the process of utilizing best-practice design methodology to create well-designed, user-friendly core values. I believe that if you design the core values to be user-friendly, they will be adopted very easily in an organization. Core values then become omnipresent in the organization. They are everywhere. They get used. They become the oxygen of the company. They define the organization—*they are the organization.*

3. CORE VALUE THEMES

What we're going to focus on first and foremost in the discovery and design process is coming up with large-scale themes that support the core beliefs of the organization. There should be no more than four or five major themes that define what the company is all about. The morning after I graduated from BOG, I realized that I needed to look at what Nurse Next Door did better than anyone else in that room full of CEOs. They had created better adoption of their core values. When I looked at their core values, I noticed that they only had four core values. This is because an organization cannot stand for everything. There should be four or five pillars of belief that the company can rally around. In the classic bestseller *Built to Last*, Jim Collins and Jerry Porras support this idea of limiting how many core values a company should have when they state the following:

> "*Visionary companies tend to only have a few core values, usually between three and six. In fact, we found none of the visionary companies to have more than six core values, and most have less. And, indeed we should expect this, for only a few values can be truly core— values so fundamental and deeply held that they will change or be compromised seldom if ever.*" *Collins and Porras further make the point,* "*This has important implications for articulating core values in your own organization. If you list more than five or six values, you might not be capturing those that are truly core.*"[9]

It's clear that companies need to pay close attention to what matters most when embarking on the core value discovery process.

I like to use the following exercise when discovering company core values.

Below is a list of 105 distinct core values. We ask the company leaders to pick the top four to five core values that they believe define the personality of the company—what the company really needs to stand for when push comes to shove. At the end of the day, there are a lot of values we live by, but four or five key themes should resonate with us above all else. Those are going to be the most important to carry the organization to its highest level. What are the four or five most important things that the organization wants to be known for? These should not be an ambitious wish list of items, rather what the company truly stands for at its core.

---

9   Jim Collins and Jerry Porras, Built to Last: Successful Habits of Visionary Companies (HarperCollins, 1994), 73-76.

Adventurous	Approachable	Assertive	Caring	Committed	Creative	Authenticity
Courageous	Attentive	Bold	Community	Consistent	Curious	Balance
Energetic	Calm	Collaborative (collaborate)	Compassionate	Dedicated	Innovative	Faith
Enthusiastic	Easy Going	Competent	Conscientious	Dependable	Inventive	Humility
Excellence	Even-tempered	Competitive	Considerate	Disciplined	Talented	Insightful
Freedom	Flexible	Confident	Empathy	Fair	Unique	Intelligent
Inspiring	Great listener	Decisive	Forgiving	Honest		Knowledgeable
Outgoing	Helpful	Determined	Friendly	Integrity		Logical
Passionate	Open-minded	Diligent	Fun-loving	Just		Mindfulness
Risk-taker	Polite	Driven	Generous	Loyal		Modest
Self-made	Prepared	Efficient	Happiness	Responsible		Optimistic
Values-driven	Present	Engaged	Humor	Steadfast		Peaceful
	Responsive	Focused	Kind	Straightforward		Pragmatic
	Service-oriented	Honor	Loving	Trustworthy		Savvy
	Sincere	Independent	Playful			Spiritual
	Thoughtful	Organized	Selfless			Well-rounded
	Tolerant	Positive	Sensitive			Wise
		Proactive				
		Productive				
		Results-oriented				
		Thorough				
		Tradition				

A few things to consider when picking the top four to five themes listed above are as follows:

1. Include one core value that encompasses how team members interact with one another. This generally reflects how team members treat customers.
2. Include one core value around what leadership looks like in the organization.
3. If one or two themes overlap, combine them into one theme. For example, Innovative and Creative would likely be under the same theme. Do not make those separate from one another, as they can coexist. This is discussed more

in chapter 5, when we discuss core value descriptives and subthemes.

4. Your top four or five themes do not have to be nice, and they should not be what you think people want you to be known for. They should represent exactly who you are as an organization.

Remember, core values don't have to be nice. There are loving and family-friendly organizations, and there are more aggressive organizations. Be true to yourself and your company when choosing your top four to five core value themes.

At my current business, The Money Source Inc. (TMS), the four core value themes that define who we are as a company are the following:

- People Matter.—Caring
- Strength of Character—Integrity
- Inspiring Leadership—Inspiring
- Rock Solid Service—Service Oriented

At my previous company, Twin Capital, the four core value themes that defined who we were as a company were the following:

- Do Work!—Productive
- Live Zen—Integrity
- Break the Box—Innovative
- Wow Everyone—Excellence

This is a great example of two mortgage companies, both in the same industry with similar ownership, but with different core values, each representing something different to the world.

From my standpoint having been the CEO of both companies, these are two very different companies, even though there is overlap when it comes to some of the highest-level leadership. When we view our companies as living, breathing organisms, with their own personalities, we start to see that there are many different elements that drive what will eventually become the core values of the organization. These elements include the makeup of the team, the location of the business, the types of leaders involved in the organization, as well as the business climate in which the company is currently living. It's essential that we take our time during the discovery process to discern which core value themes truly represent the company.

CONCLUSION

The most crucial takeaway from this chapter is the importance of quality design thinking when creating your core values. Core values define your company culture and personality: your products, your everyday functioning, your customers' experiences. Steve Jobs's father built a fence that lasted fifty years, and Steve Jobs wove design into all aspects of Apple to make it one of the largest organizations today—good design withstands the test of time. Good design needs to be simple and user-friendly if you want to see mass adoption and long-term use. The next step is to discover the top four to five core value themes that define the personality of the company—what the company really needs to stand for when push comes to shove. They don't have to be nice; they need to be authentic and true to the company. This is the first mile in the marathon of the core value discovery and design process. In the next chapters, we will explore shaping these themes into well-designed and fully functional core values. The goal is to create core values that will be widely adopted and used in your company for decades to come.

PART 2

CHAPTER 5

HOW TO BUILD CORE VALUES

"The Magic number 7 (plus or minus two) provides evidence for the capacity of short-term memory. Most adults can store between 5 and 9 items in their short-term memory. This idea was put forward by Miller (1956) and he called it the magic number 7."[10]

The passage above is a description of a phenomenon in psychology known as Miller's law. It says that we, as humans, have the capacity to store seven items (plus or minus two) in our short-term memory for easy access. A great example of Miller's law at work would be the act of remembering a phone number. It is easy to remember a phone number off the top of your head. However, if I ask you to remember two different phone numbers at the same time, the results are usually not good. This is an important idea when designing your core values. When I sat down at BOG in 2008, I was surrounded by fifty-seven of

---

10 G. Miller, "The Magical Number Seven, Plus or Minus Two: Some Limits on Our Capacity for Processing Information," *Psychological Review* 63 (1956): 81–97.

the best core-value-driven entrepreneurs in the world, yet they all sat down when it came to them and their teams knowing their core values. How could that be? We have established that if you, as the leader, don't know your core values off the top of your head and your team does not know them off the top of their heads, then your core values are not alive and well in your organization.

This is where the design process matters when building a core-value-driven organization. If you and your team need to easily remember the core values, then the first thing you need to do is make them easy to remember. This is where Miller's law comes into play. Based on Miller's law, the core values should be no more than seven items to remember, plus or minus two. So, five to nine items is the ideal number to make the items memorable.

We then need to decide what we want people to remember. I have designed a four-part architecture for core value design known as the Core Value Waterfall.

THE CORE VALUE WATERFALL

1. **Pick your theme**. From the 105 core value themes, pick the top four or five themes that define the personality of the company—what the company really needs to stand for when push comes to shove.
2. **The header**. These are your top four to five themes translated into sticky, memorable, user-friendly words and phrases. The only thing we want people to remember off the top of their heads are the headers. These must be easily memorized and remembered by the team.
3. **The descriptive**. This is four to six sentences that the leadership and the team use to describe what each core value

means in detail. The descriptive gives transparency and clarity on how we define what the header truly means to the organization. This does not need to be memorized or remembered off the top of anyone's head. This can always be referenced and needs to be understood by the team and the leadership of the organization. We will also dive deep into the design of the descriptive utilizing the following best practices:

A. Descriptive length
B. Thou shalt not have products
C. 100-year rule
D. Best team member rule
E. Never again
F. Subthemes
G. Positivity only
H. Scenario testing

4. **Core value policy and procedures**. This is a living document that dives deep into how the core values are used tactically in the business. This can change as the company, products, and the world around us change. Think of this as your standard operating procedures and policy and procedure in your company. This also does not need to be memorized.

I like to think of the design process as the following when building core values:

- Core value theme: Thirty-thousand-foot level
- Core value descriptive: Ten-thousand-foot level
- Core value policy and procedures: Ground level

The theme is the largest overarching idea that we are trying to level up to. The descriptive gives details as to what the theme looks like in practice, while staying out of the details. The policy and procedures are a tactical document spelling out the details of what the descriptive looks like in every facet of the organization. Keep these levels in mind while going through the Core Value Waterfall.

Let's now dive deep into each part of the Core Value Waterfall. To start with, let's look at our core value themes.

1. PICK YOUR THEME

The first thing to do is figure out the top four or five themes that define the personality of the company. What are the most important themes that the company wants to stand for when push comes to shove? In chapter 4, we looked at 105 different core value themes. You will want to spend time with the senior leadership team to do a discovery process to decide what these top four to five core values truly are. Do not worry about how they are going to be presented to the outside world at this point. The goal here is to really focus on what is most important to the organization. Don't rush this part of the process. It takes time and energy to get this right.

As a reminder, there are four rules to follow when narrowing down the 105 different core value themes into the top four to five themes:

1. Include one core value that encompasses how team members interact with one another. This generally also reflects how team members treat customers.
2. Include one core value around what leadership looks like in the organization.
3. If one or two themes overlap, combine them into one theme.

For example, Innovative and Creative would likely be under the same theme. Do not make those separate from one another, as they can coexist. We will delve deeper into this later in the chapter.

4. The top four or five themes do not have to be nice and they should not be what you think people want you to be known for. They should represent exactly who you are as an organization.

Now that you have your top four to five themes, let's move on to the header.

2. THE HEADER

The header is one of the most important parts of the core value design process. It is what we want our organization to be known for. This is where the themes come to life in the organization. At TMS, we landed on the following themes when we went through the process of discovering our core values:

- Caring
- Integrity
- Inspiration
- Service Oriented

These were the four most important core values that we wanted to promote inside and outside the business. They are what we are willing to fall on our sword for. Once we had the themes picked out, the next step was to apply Miller's law to bring these four themes to life. We used five to nine keywords to make these four themes memorable within the organization. *(Note: when we are choosing the five to nine keywords, we are not counting articles and prepositions such as "the," "a," "an," "of," "to," "with," "in," "on," "for," "at," "with," "by," etc. The main idea here is that the five to nine keywords we use stand out and represent the essence of the core value theme that we have landed on. I will refer to the keywords as "items" for purposes of clarity.)*

When we use these five to nine items effectively, the core values have a much better likeliness of being remembered. This will aid in the core values coming to life in the organization. In the case of TMS, we did the following:

Caring = **People Matter. (Two items: "People" and "Matter")** We landed on this at a time when the mortgage industry had just survived the 2008 subprime implosion. The industry shrank by over 75 percent during the years 2008 to 2011. By 2013, things were just coming back to life and those who had survived in our industry had a bad taste in their mouths after living through five exhausting and painful years. The workforce in the industry had been marginalized and treated like second-class citizens. We knew we could be a change agent by leading with this core value in our company. It is very important for us to have a company where we all care about one another. We believe that our people are our most valuable asset. We knew that we had to have a theme that really exemplified this core value. (Note: we use a period at the end of the words *People Matter* to emphasize the importance of this sentiment.)

Integrity = **Strength of Character (Two items: "Strength" and "Character")** We chose integrity as a core value of our company, as our industry had imploded due to a lack of integrity from 2001 to 2007. The mortgage industry put its values aside and made toxic subprime loans that took down the world economy. *We'll be damned if we ever have to deal with something like that again.* We wanted to stand tall and proud around the idea that we do the right things at our company. Integrity was, and still is, a nonnegotiable core value at TMS.

Inspiration = **Inspiring Leadership (Two items: "Inspiring" and "Leadership")** This is important to us, as we know that people in the company must be able to look toward one another, **regardless of position or rank**, to be inspired. It also communicates to our team that everyone is a leader in the organization, regardless of title, and that we should look to one another for inspiration if we are to elevate the organization to the highest of standards. We also know that we are in a service business and that our people are our biggest investment and asset. In order to be a company that puts our people first and invests in them, we need to have a culture that celebrates inspiration. This is a natural ingredient that supercharges our first core value, "People Matter." We know that this creates a standard for our managers when they are interacting with their team. It is explicit, and they know what the organization expects from them.

Service Oriented = **Rock Solid Service (Three items: "Rock," "Solid," and "Service")** We want our team and customers to know that we are a culture that is service oriented and that the type of service we provide is important. Hence the words "ROCK SOLID." We want them to see that the client should love us and become a raving fan. We put this out into the world, not because we expect perfection (as there are always potential service issues in every business and organization), but because, when things falter, we want a north star that says that we expect our team to provide awesome service. The goal here is to create a benchmark for everyone's expectations. We expect our team members to move toward and above that benchmark.

So, let's do the math:

- People Matter. (two items)
- Strength of Character (two items)
- Inspiring Leadership (two items)
- Rock Solid Service (three items)

....

Nine items total

Success! Our core values fit Miller's law. We had nine items, and we allowed for a maximum of nine! Score one for TMS's core values. Remember, if you can't remember the header, then you are not creating a core value that is designed and positioned for mass adoption in your organization. This is the first step to success in our core value design methodology. Again, four to five themes maximum, not exceeding nine items in total, for all the headers.

Most organizations get this wrong. They try to do too much when they are building their core values. They do not have the end user in mind when they build their core values. The result they end up with is a set of core values that are not built to be used in the organization. Think of your company. If I pulled aside ten random employees in your organization, how many are likely to be able to tell me all the company's core values off the top of their heads? If I asked *you* to tell me *your* company's core values off the top of *your* head, how many would *you* get right? Think of this as an elevator pitch—if you can't explain your business in ten seconds or less, it means your business plan has issues. If you can't tell me your core values off the top of your head, it means your core value design has issues.

When we have too many words in our core values, we increase

the likeliness that no one in the organization will be able to remember these core values without having to reference a piece of paper. At best, they will be partially adopted in the organization and, at worst, they will simply become a cultural ruin. Think of a cultural ruin as something that people visit during their hiring process and possibly during reviews, but that serve very little function in the day-to-day use of the business. If you and your staff cannot remember your core values, then how are these values ever going to come to life in the organization?

At TMS we were very intentional about the design of our core values. Using Miller's law, we have turned our top four themes into very memorable core value headers:

- Caring = **People Matter.**
- Integrity = **Strength of Character**
- Inspiration = **Inspiring Leadership**
- Service Oriented = **Rock Solid Service**

Have fun with this part of the process. This is where you start to get creative with making the core values come to life. These words or phrases should reflect who you are as an organization. The words that you choose should fit the tone of the organization and the leadership. If you are silly and fun, choose fun and silly words to reflect the theme. If you are more tough and serious, make them more tough and serious. Words matter, and the words you choose reflect who you are in the world. This is important in the design of your core value headers. They should reflect exactly what these themes mean. You should also try to make them catchy and memorable. This is how we help people remember things. The key to this part of the process is the same as the key to deciding the themes: be authentic to the voice of your organization. This will help to attract people with personal core values that resonate with your organization. You also don't want to be boring here. This is a common mistake. It's not to say that people won't remember your core values if they are boring; you are just leaving some money on the table regarding expressing your organization's voice to your team.

For instance, I could have kept the following as my four core values at TMS:

- Caring
- Integrity
- Inspiration
- Service Oriented

These five words are super easy to remember. But they are not interesting. They don't tell you anything about the voice of the company. They don't tell you that we are fun and forward-thinking. They don't tell you that we put a lot of pressure on ourselves to be the best. This is what I mean about leaving money on the table. When I put some thought into the words and express the tone and voice of the organization, then these five words transform into our core value headers that we know and love at TMS:

- People Matter.
- Strength of Character
- Inspiring Leadership
- Rock Solid Service

Can you see the difference? Words matter. Use them judiciously and make them count. If you can do this with your core value headers and apply Miller's law in the process, you have just set up your core values to be able to come alive in your organization.

3. THE DESCRIPTIVE

This is the four to six sentences that the leadership and the team use to describe what the core value means in detail. Each descriptive offers transparency and clarity regarding what the theme truly means to the organization. This **does not need to be memorized** or remembered off the top of anyone's head. This can always be referenced and needs to be understood in general terms by the team and the leadership of the organization.

The descriptive is used for all decision-making in the organization. Word choice and sentence structure are extremely important when building your descriptive. This is important because words are very nuanced and can have more than one meaning. Sentence structure is very intricate and can communicate a particular tone. Therefore, it is important to define exactly what the core value looks like in your organization, and to be as specific as possible so that there is no room for confusion. Allow me to illustrate using our core value of "People Matter."

"People Matter." is all about the core value of Caring—specifically, caring for the people of our company. This value alone, without a specific descriptive, can be interpreted in many ways depending on who the reader is.

If I am a client, it could mean that "I matter." If I am an employee, it could mean that we as the team matter. If I am a manager, it could mean that the leadership is who matters. If I am the owner, it could mean that the owner matters. All these different constituents' needs may be at odds with one another at certain times. So, who matters then? The descriptive helps to elaborate on what this means to us as an organization. It is meant to be very specific and to aid in the use of the value as far as comprehension is concerned. Remember, the purpose of the core values is to establish a baseline for expectation. This tells everyone what we stand for as an organization, and it provides guardrails so that everyone knows what they need to do to meet these expectations. The descriptive is a paragraph of four to six sentences. It looks at the organization from a ten-thousand-foot level. The descriptive should paint a concrete picture of what the core value looks like when it is alive and well.

The goal of the descriptive is to promote the best behavior within the company. It should eliminate any conduct in the organization that questions the integrity of the values. The descriptive is a filter for decision-making. Every decision that needs to be made should be answered in the descriptive. When I say every decision, I mean *every* decision.

My business partners and I have had some very hard decisions to make at TMS. I found that when we were challenged with our hardest decisions, our core values came to the rescue. By reading the core values out loud along with the descriptives, we have never faced a problem where we did not know what to do. The core values always give you the answer. I can admit that I've not always liked what the core values have said I have to do. However, it is always very clear what decision we need to make if the core values are to be alive and well in the organization.

When I sat in the diner in Cambridge, Massachusetts, on that fateful morning in 2008, I remember thinking that I had to make the descriptives say what we were going to look like as an organization. I started writing a list of what the core values should look like so that I could have the right people on the bus and make sure the wrong people would get off. I decided that the descriptives need to be built so that the core values cannot be used against the company. This is what I now call the *weaponization of the core values*. Here is an example.

Below are the new and improved core values that I designed for Twin Capital that morning in Cambridge:

Do Work!

- We value individuals who love their jobs and work their hardest to make our firm stand out above our competition.
- We work hard, make the best use of our time, and maximize the effects of all of our actions.
- We value great work ethic in all of our team members.
- We do not confuse effort with results; we are a results-driven organization.

Live Zen

- We believe in the inevitable outcomes of both good and bad karma.
- We only want team members with extremely positive attitudes.
- We make lemonade from lemons.
- The glass is always half full.
- We strive to create positive connections with all clients, team members, and business partners in our organization.
- We promote positive energy through our work, family, and communities that we impact through our business.
- We believe in teamwork and the power of cohesive positive energy.
- Through our belief in karma, we are always able to protect our firm.

Break the Box

- We strive to find a better, easier way to do our work.
- We attract people who are not confined by their job title, job description, or daily responsibilities to make us a better organization.
- We are creative thinkers who are not afraid to take risks in coming up with a better way to conduct our business.
- We utilize technology for simple, easier, more cost-effective outcomes.
- If it is not broken, don't fix it; use it and make it better.
- We strive to stay ahead of the curve through creative strategic thinking.

Wow Everyone

- We strive to create the best experience possible for our clients, team members, vendors, and business partners.
- We are a team that is always raising the bar in terms of customer service and client experience with our firm.
- We go above and beyond the call of duty to our clients and team members.
- We recognize that multiple team members contribute to the job at hand and, through respect and extraordinary effort, we are able to perform at higher and higher levels.
- We strive to have people brag about their experience with our firm.
- Our end goal is to create a world-class team who provides world-class customer service.

About a year after I rolled out the new core values, I had the first exchange with a team member who attempted to weaponize the core values and use them against the company. A gentleman by the name of Carl, who worked for us at Twin Capital, was an interesting guy. He was in his early fifties and was a nice enough fella. He was from Minnesota and had lived in California for about fifteen years. Carl was a stereotypical lifelong sales guy. Carl was a bit ADD, quirky, and liked to rock 1980s Def Leppard T-shirts with their sleeves cut off to our office get-togethers. The man wore jean shorts. I think you know the type of person I am describing. Carl had a bit of used car salesman in him. He was also our lowest producer in the company and, for this reason, we decided that we would not give him our best leads anymore. We had new leads that cost the company $100 to $150 per lead. We also had an aged database of these same leads that had not converted, which we called "the Wood." When salespeople's conversion rates were not high enough, we would stop giving them the new, expensive leads and they would only get access to the Wood. We called this "Working the Wood." Carl had been a few weeks into Working the Wood and was not very happy about this. However, we were not happy with the ROI we were getting on our investment in Carl as a salesperson. Working the Wood was the only option he had if he wanted to stay in our company, at least until his numbers picked up. One day, Carl asked to have a meeting with me about this situation, and we scheduled it for just after lunch that day.

"You know," Carl said when he sat down, "I am really concerned about the company."

"Why is that?" I asked.

"I am concerned that the company is not living our core values right now."

Well, that was concerning. "Why would you think that?"

"As you know, I have not gotten any fresh leads for a while, and I think that the company is not living our core value of Live Zen."

Here is our core value of Live Zen, as well as the descriptive:

Live Zen

- We believe in the inevitable outcomes of both good and bad karma.
- We only want team members with extremely positive attitudes.
- We make lemonade from lemons.
- The glass is always half full.
- We strive to create positive connections with all clients, team members, and business partners in our organization.
- We promote positive energy through our work, family, and communities that we impact through our business.
- We believe in teamwork and the power of cohesive positive energy.
- Through our belief in karma, we are always able to protect our firm.

Nowhere in this descriptive does it reference us as an organization giving low producers leads. Carl was not the sharpest tool in the shed, but this is a great example of the weaponization of the core values by a core value misfit. Yes, Carl was a core value misfit. I used this as an opportunity to go on the offense with Carl. When the core values are designed well, they are positioned so that the company can turn the tables on those who decide to use the values against the organization.

"Well," I said to Carl, "here is where we can agree to disagree. The real issue is that your production is why you are getting the leads you are getting. As you know, we have four core values at Twin Capital. Although you may believe that we are not Living Zen by not giving you leads, I believe that if you were living our other three core values—meaning you Do Work!, Break the Box, and Wow Everyone—then I would feel more inclined to give you the leads you are asking for. The fact of the matter is that these things have not happened, and, for that reason, I cannot give you the leads you want."

Carl decided to leave the company not too long after this conversation. He had self-selected out, despite his efforts to weaponize the core values against the company. When core values are alive and well in an organization, your misfits will try to use them against you. This is why it is essential that the descriptives do the following: describe how you want to look at the world, who can be in the organization, and who must either never join or leave the company. When designed properly, the descriptives should give everyone in the company the answer to any question or decision that needs to be made. This is why I believe that core values are the most powerful tool an organization can possess when designed, implemented, and brought to life.

Descriptives are important and embody the best practices needed to execute the core values. Deciding what this content should be is critical. The descriptives cannot change in the future, they should be designed to answer any question that exists in the organization, and they need to be relevant as your company pivots, iterates, and ages in your respective and future marketplaces. I will now cover eight best practices to position your descriptives for maximum impact.

A. Descriptive Length

I have found that, when designing the descriptives, four to six sentences seem to be the right amount of information. This allows your core value headers and descriptives to fit on one piece of paper, one wall, and one business card. You can get your point across without overwhelming the user. It forces the organization to stay at the ten-thousand-foot level. It also allows you to be detailed enough to cover your bases. Think of the four to six items that the core values need to say to be alive and well when tested from a decision-making standpoint. Simply put: keep your descriptives to four to six sentences max, and no more than one paragraph. You will have the core value policy and procedures to go deep into the tactical use of the core values in the daily life of your organization.

Again, think of the core values as such:

- Core value theme: Thirty-thousand-foot level
- Core value descriptive: Ten-thousand-foot level
- Core value policy and procedures: Ground level

B. Thou Shalt Not Have Products

The next big mistake I see many organizations make when creating descriptives is including their products and services in their core value descriptives. This is very tactical and shortsighted. You do not want to be the guy talking about buggy whips or VHS cassettes or CDs or Walkmans (shall I go on?) in your core values. Products have no place in your core values. Remember, this is all about stating what the organization stands for—the type of people, customers, team members, and behavior you want to see in the organization. This drives decisions that shape your products and services. Products and services should not be anywhere near your descriptives. This is a massive "no-no" in core value design and sets you up for failure; it undermines the architecture of the core values and how they are used in the long term in the organization.

C. One-Hundred-Year Rule

Speaking of long-term use, our golden rule is this: your core values should be just as relevant one hundred years from now as they are today. Yes, you heard me correctly: your core value theme and descriptive should not age out. If you stay high level— that is, thirty thousand feet for the theme and ten thousand feet for the descriptive—and you do not allow product to find its way into the design process, you should be fine. Your core values should never be able to change. I know what some of you are thinking: there could be a new CEO, times change, people change. I could not disagree more. These statements mean that either the core values were not designed properly, or they were not applied and used properly.

A good example is a conversation I had with a friend of mine who is a leader of an amazing management consulting firm. He was promoting the idea that you can change your core values as needed, with which I respectfully disagreed. He and I had a chance to discuss his position, and I told him that I believed that core values should never change in an organization. He then challenged me on this, using himself as an example.

"Well, Darius, when I was a young man, I used to like to go out and party with my friends. Now I am a father and husband, and I don't do those things anymore."

"Friend," I said, "I will make the argument that your values are the same; however, your application of your values has changed (descriptive versus policy and procedure). It sounds to me that you have core values around relationship building. In the past, you chose to spend your time building relationships with your friends in a way that involved socializing, partying, and having a good time. Now you choose to spend that time building relationships with your wife and children that involve being a great husband and father. The core value is the same; the application is what has changed."

"Touché," my friend said.

But he did not let up and challenged me even further.

"I see what you are saying about my core values, but I will challenge this in another way. I have a client that is a seventy-five-year-old billion-dollar manufacturing company. The CEO has brought in his son-in-law to run the company and he is really shaking things up. His son-in-law is a big-data guy and is trying to redesign the core values around becoming a technology-driven organization. They have always been a 'look you in the eye and shake your hand' type of company, and this is ruffling a lot of feathers. Many of their long-term employees are having issues with the change in the company and are not adjusting to this new way of doing business very well. I would argue that their core values have changed and that being innovative and tech-driven is a new core value for them."

"What are their core values?" I asked.

"Hard work, caring about their team, integrity, and winning."

The answer was simple. "I am going to make the argument that using technology and innovation is all about their core value of *winning*. How they get there may have changed (policy and procedures), but the act of wanting to *win* is universal and timeless. Their core values have not changed; their people are having issues with the new *way* of winning."

Core values should be timeless. A life well-lived is one that is aligned and supported by one's values. Your core value theme and descriptive should never change. This is why there needs to be time and attention invested in the discovery and design process.

This is the premise of the one-hundred-year rule. The core values of the organization should withstand the test of time. They should be just as relevant ten, twenty, thirty, fifty, and even one hundred years from now, regardless of the products sold or the customers served. When this happens, you have truly defined what the organization stands for in the most meaningful of ways.

D. Best Team Member Rule

One of my favorite secrets for creating great descriptives is writing a list of the best team members who are either still in the organization or the people I have worked with in the past that truly embody the company's core values. Think of your superstars. Think of the people who you wish you had many more of. Think of the people who are alumni of your company who you would take back in a heartbeat. These are your core value rock stars and we all have them in our organizations.

Once you have identified a list of exceptional individuals who you wished you could clone, you then need to identify a list of reasons why you love working with them. What makes them so great? What resonates for you when you think about the things you love about having them on your team? What makes them exceptional? What actions do you see them commit to naturally that make you proud? What makes them stand out? In my first company, Twin Capital, we had this as our number-one core value:

Do Work!

- We value individuals who love their jobs and work their hardest to make our firm stand out above all of our competition.
- We work hard, make the best use of our time, and maximize the effects of all of our actions.
- We value great work ethic in all of our team members.
- We do not confuse effort with results; we are a results-driven organization.

When I was crafting this core value descriptive, I thought of the people at Twin Capital who truly embodied this value. We had four individuals who stood out. They all loved what they did, put the company first, were results-oriented, and had amazing work ethic. When I was crafting the descriptive for DO WORK! I thought about the attributes of these core value rock stars. I then made sure that the things I loved about working with them were represented in the descriptive. To this day, more than ten years later, I still see each one of them and the contributions they made to Twin Capital in the core value of DO WORK!

The core values are a tool that guides all decision-making in your organization. One of the biggest decisions we make as leaders is deciding who we bring into our company. The goal is to find people who believe what we believe. Inversely, the core values should be a filter for folks to either self-select out or be asked to leave an organization when there is a core value misfit.

E. Never Again

"Never Again" is all about blocking the people who are the *opposite* of your *best team member*. These are people who you would *never* want to work with again. Just as you did with the *best team member*, you want to make a list of these folks and go through the same process. Who are the people whom you would never want to have in your organization ever again? What made you feel this way about them? Why are these people so misaligned with the company? You want to focus on the top two to three people. Try to stay away from opinion here; you want to focus on the core issues. I will give you an example.

In a former life, I was involved in a joint venture where I saw this concept play out. About one year into the joint venture, there was a reorganization of the business and a new CEO (let's call her Sarah) was brought in to replace the current CEO of the company. Sarah made many promises to the existing management team. The problem was that the actions that followed did not align with what was said. There were many inconsistencies. Over the course of the next eight months, I left the company, as did every other manager in my group, for this reason. When my partners and I built the core values at TMS, we specifically wanted to make sure that this type of behavior would not be part of our business. We wanted to make sure that a person like this could never stay at a company like ours. We included a sentence in our Inspiring Leadership core value to protect us from this ever happening:

Inspiring Leadership

Our leaders lead from the front lines and are involved at all levels. While promoting personal accountability and independent thinking, our leadership has the ability to recognize what is needed and is eager to jump in and roll up their sleeves. Our leaders know that leading is about listening and caring for our employees. The satisfaction of our customers is directly related to the happiness of our employees, and we work to create positive environments. **We believe that actions are the only truth.** We strive to be true by consistently modeling and living by TMS's vision and creating a culture of high performance, transparency, and accountability.

We included the line "We believe that actions are the only truth" because we knew we had to make sure a person like Sarah could never be part of our business. It was specific to what we had seen Sarah and some of her direct reports do at our previous company—we were very sensitive to how it negatively affected both us and the other managers that were on the receiving end of this type of behavior. It rubbed us the wrong way.

Another example is a manager (let's call him David) at Twin Capital. David was a great producer but was consistently negative. He was known for putting people down and speaking about things in a negative light. It brought everyone's mood down. On one end of the spectrum, he lived our core value of Do Work! He had an amazing work ethic and was extremely productive. On the other end of the spectrum, he was a negative person—I would get anxious when he would come into my office, before he even said a word. I knew that a positive attitude was an important part of what we wanted in our company, regardless of how great someone might be at their job. So, when we were crafting the core value of Live Zen, we made sure that the descriptive disallowed David from ever working with us in the future.

Live Zen

- We believe in the inevitable outcomes of both good and bad karma.
- **We only want team members with extremely positive attitudes.**
- We make lemonade from lemons.
- **The glass is always half full.**
- We strive to create positive connections with all clients, team members, and business partners in our organization.
- We promote positive energy through our work, family, and communities that we impact through our business.
- We believe in teamwork and the power of cohesive positive energy.
- Through our belief in karma, we are always able to protect our firm.

David was so difficult to work with that we wrote *two* sentences to make sure someone like him could not be a part of our organization in the future:

- **We only want team members with extremely positive attitudes.**
- **The glass is always half full.**

The key here is to make sure that we fill our organizations with core value rock stars and block or remove core value misfits. The core values should be a strong filter for both good and bad fits in the organization.

F. Subthemes

The descriptives are a great place to capture the subthemes you honed in on when narrowing down your top four to five core value themes. Through the core value theme selection process, ten to twenty themes are chosen before narrowing them down to four to five. These five to fifteen core value themes that remain should not be wasted. These themes are also important in shaping and prioritizing core values in the company. They may not be in the top five; however, they are still core values that are important to defining who you are as an organization.

There is a great place to use these core value themes. I call them subthemes. You want to bucket these under the main themes and see what resonates. For example, let's say you land on the following four core values as your most important core values:

1. Courageous
2. Calm
3. Bold
4. Kind

And you have the following subthemes (#5–20)

5. Inspiring
6. Passionate
7. Excellence
8. Present
9. Sincere
10. Organized
11. Positive
12. Friendly
13. Humor
14. Responsible

15. Disciplined
16. Inventive
17. Modest
18. Wise
19. Productive
20. Fun-loving

The first thing you want to do is look for similar themes and put them under a core value bucket. (You can use a subtheme more than once if you want.)

- Courageous: Inspiring, passionate
- Calm: Present, modest
- Bold: Disciplined, inspiring
- Kind: Positive, friendly

Next, you want to think of how this core value looks when it is alive and well in the company. For instance, take the value of "Courageous" or the act of showing courage. What are some ways that I see the core value of "Courageous" being lived in the company?

Courageous:

- We show courage by showing passion (**passionate**).
- We are **inspiring** to those around us.
- We expect **excellence**, even when things are not going our way.
- We show courage by being **modest**, even when we have every right to show off.
- We show courage by having a sense of **humor** in the face of adversity.
- We show courage by being **inventive** in a tough and competitive industry despite the odds of success.

You get the point. When you narrow in on the top twenty core values, you will have elements of your descriptives in those top twenty. They may not be the top four or five themes, but they are still able to influence those top four or five core value themes. By weaving the next ten to fifteen themes into the descriptive of the top four or five core value themes, we give body and depth to what is important to the organization. In the case of "Courageous," we get to be this by exhibiting the subthemes of passion, inspiration, excellence, modesty, humor, and by being inventive. *Yes*, you can now have your cake and eat it too!

G. Positivity Only

One of the golden rules of a great descriptive is keeping it positive. You should never have negative statements in your core values. It should never be "We are not…" statements or "We never…" or "At ACME company, we do not…" These types of statements can always be made into a positive. Let's use the example of my Inspiring Leadership core value from TMS and not wanting to work with someone like Sarah again. In the descriptive for Inspiring Leadership we use a very powerful sentence: "We believe that actions are the only truth."

We easily could have said "We do not allow liars to join our company" or "We believe that if your actions are not aligned with your statements, then you do not fit our company culture." Both are negative ways of saying the statement we chose to make: "We believe that actions are the only truth." The core values should be uplifting. Never point at what you **don't** want. Point at what you **do** want in the descriptive, and establish that as the standard. Always make sure the statements and core values are positive!

H. Scenario Testing

The last rule of building great core value descriptives is to scenario test your core values. The easiest way to do this is to come up with a list of the biggest and toughest decisions you have had to make as a company over the past few months or year. You will want to state this problem out loud, and then you will need to read the core values and their descriptives out loud. After this, you should ask yourself and the leaders who are in the room a very simple question:

What do the core values say that we need to do regarding this decision?

If the answer is not clear, this means that you have holes in your core value descriptives. You will need to add another element to address this in the appropriate core value. The core values should give you clear direction on every decision that needs to be made in the organization. If they fail to do this, then there is likely something missing in the core value themes or descriptives. There is a bit of trial and error involved with this; however, well-designed core values should address all problems.

Remember:

CORE VALUES = DECISIONS = ACTIONS = RESULTS

4. CORE VALUE POLICY AND PROCEDURES

Remember the different levels I mentioned earlier in the chapter?

- Core value theme: Thirty-thousand-foot level
- Core value descriptive: Ten-thousand-foot level
- Core value policy and procedures: Ground level

Once you have the themes and descriptives designed and built, you will want to consider the core value policy and procedures. This is the area where you have the most flexibility. You can go crazy here. Be as specific as you want. You should include products, processes, standard operating procedures, service-level agreements—have at it. The core value policy and procedures are just like any traditional policies and procedures you would have in a company. The key difference is that they are framed utilizing the language and beliefs outlined in the core values that you have built into your company. Think of the core value policy and procedures as bringing the core values to life in every policy and procedure in your organization. This can be a very interesting proposition as you start to look at your current policy and procedures. You may see that there are gaps between what your current policy and procedures tell the team members to do versus what the core values say that they should do. Fun stuff, I know. The point is to make sure you align from the highest (thirty-thousand-foot) level all the way down to how it translates into the day-to-day ground-level behavior, functions, and processes of the organization. If there are gaps, fix them. If you need to make the policy more specific to ensure that the policy protects what is stated in the core value, then please do so. You will need to make sure that your core values line up from top to bottom, and your core value policy and procedures allow you to do this. At TMS, we saw early on that our core value of "Rock Solid Service" was being broken by how we were conducting some of our business practices, as well as how we were interacting with each other internally. People would not respond to each other's emails, ignore clients, and fall into bad habits that they likely had before adopting the core value of "Rock Solid Service." It was very frustrating, so I decided that we needed to do something about it.

At this point, the core values had been rolled out in the

organization for about three to four months. I pulled every employee aside and addressed them in groups of seven to eight people.

"Guys, we have the core value of Rock Solid Service in our company. We have service issues both internally and externally. It is clear to me that we are not living this core value. In fact, we just conducted our NPS and we are at 31 percent. We are way better than that. I am going to ask you guys to help me out here."

I then hung up a couple of those large Post-its on the wall.

"For the next thirty days, you guys can write on these Post-its exactly what needs to happen for Rock Solid Service to be alive and well in our organization. I will not tell you what the policies and procedures need to be. You tell me."

That was that. Thirty days came and went and, when all was said and done, I was able to create two distinct policies and procedures based on the input I received from the team.

The best part of this process is it was their ideas and their words. I was not dictating to them what needed to be done; they were telling each other what their actions and behavior needed to look like in the business. We were then able to create and implement the following policy and procedures to hold the team accountable to our core value of Rock Solid Service:

Rock Solid Service Policy and Procedure

TMS strives to build a raving fan base through consistent service, quality products, and accessibility. We recognize that many team members contribute to our endeavor. Through respect and extraordinary effort, we are able to perform at higher and higher levels. We set ourselves apart from every other organization with our commitment to quality, competence, consistency, and kindness.

How Do We Create Rock Solid Customer Service?

The question we must always ask ourselves when it comes to delivering **ROCK SOLID SERVICE**: "Are your actions resulting in the client choosing to interact with you and TMS **again**?"

By being mindful of the following ROCKS, regardless of position, we ensure that we are living our core values and delivering Rock Solid Service:

- **ROCK #1**—UPODU—Under Promise Over Deliver, with Urgency!
- **ROCK #2**—Be Proactive with Your Communication
  - Clients should not have to ask if you already know the answer.
- **ROCK #3**—Respectful Communication and Actions at All Times!
  - Check your ego at the door!
  - No finger pointing.
  - Your coworkers are not speed bumps for the bus.
- **ROCK #4**—Own Your Job or Direct Traffic
  - Knowledge is power.
  - If you don't know the answer, you need to know where to find it and direct traffic to the proper destination.
- **ROCK #5**—Have a Smile in Your Voice at All Times!
- **ROCK #6**—Do NOT Create **Unnecessary** Work for Others with Your Actions
- **ROCK #7**—Be Professional

- Leave your personal matters at home.
- We are a TEAM, not Ops vs. Sales or vice versa!
- Two wrongs don't make a right.
- **ROCK #8**—Transparency with Communication
  - Say what you mean; mean what you say.
  - Don't leave people wondering.
  - Bad news is better than no news.
  - No MUTE.
  - Using the response "No, nope, niet, nada, etc." is not an acceptable answer. We give solutions.

We also developed our communication policy and procedure since communication is so important to creating Rock Solid Service.

Rock Solid Communication Policy and Procedure

It is imperative to the success of our organization that we are able to communicate in an efficient and respectful manner. In order to do so, we are implementing the following communication policy and procedures:

1. K.I.S.S.—"Keep It Simple Special"
   A. Do not write the great American novel.
   B. If more than 3 lines, you should probably pick up the phone or request a call.
2. How to use TO, CC, and REPLY ALL
   A. TO: Write the names of the people who you expect to respond to the email.
   B. CC: Write the names of the people who need to know, but do not need to respond, also known as an FYI.
   C. If your manager, or the manager of the recipient, is included on the email, you are now escalating the issue.

- ∘ **NOTE:** When you escalate, you are telling the person you are communicating with that they are not capable of doing their job.
- ∘ **NOTE:** People do not like to be told that they are not doing their job.
  D. Only escalate after diligently trying to work out the issue with your teammate.
  E. SAY **NO** to **Hyper CCing**. What is Hyper CCing? Hyper CCing is adding more people than necessary to any one email.
  F. Only escalate when absolutely necessary; don't undermine your teammates.
  G. See escalation policy for more details on best practices on how to escalate.
  H. When escalating to your manager, make sure your manager is on the TO: line.
  I. Managers should never be on the CC: line unless they have asked you to add them for the specific issue and/or they have directed you to add them to the CC: line. This should be very rare.
  J. Reply All indicates you are replying to every individual who has received the original message. Please take special care to avoid this, unless it is your intention. It can be unnecessary and embarrassing.
3. Proper Formatting
  A. ALL CAPS = SCREAMING, and this goes against our core values. **NEVER COMMUNICATE IN ALL CAPS!!!!!**
  B. Excessive use of punctuation is unnecessary. Although we understand, at times, you may be very excited, please use your best judgment.
4. No Divorced Parents
  A. Please use the escalation policy; do not fish for answers

by asking two managers the same question until you get the answer you want. Please do not do this over email.

    B. Never duplicate communication—i.e., send the same exact question to two separate managers without them knowing that the other person received the same email.

    C. In almost every scenario, you should only be emailing your direct manager.

5. Nobody Likes a Tattletale

    A. In nearly all situations, this is inappropriate. Remember, we are a solutions-oriented company.

6. Leave Negativity at Home

    A. Give your partners, managers, and teammates solutions.

    B. No venting or criticism over email.

    C. Use 15Five and your phone for constructive criticism.

7. Professional Courtesy

    A. We are all professionals; please act like one at all times while interfacing with teammates.

8. Assume Best Intentions

    A. This is so easy, yet so hard to do sometimes. Please try your best.

9. Watch Your Tone—Especially with Email

    A. Remember email has no tone; many emails come across as impolite, even if this was never the intent of the sender. Keep this in mind while you read and write emails; it goes both ways.

10. 8 or Above Only!

    A. Do not ever send an email when you are feeling anything less than an 8 on a sanity scale of 1–10.

    B. If you are angry, frustrated, short-changed, underappreciated, devalued, or just want to have a meltdown and scream, STOP. Walk away from the computer and take a breath or 10 or 100 before you begin to think of emailing or calling anyone or anything. An email written while in an emotional state can cause a ton of heartache for you later on.

c. **Front Page of the *New York Times***: A simple question to ask yourself: Would you be proud of that email if it was put on the front page of the *New York Times*? If the answer is NO...then please do not send the email.

A few weeks later, I saw a manager not living the core value of "Inspiring Leadership" in our organization. I then created a core value policy and procedure to outline exactly what this was to look like in our organization.[11]

Once we rolled out the core value policy and procedures, we saw an overnight turnaround in our NPS and in the way the team worked together. By putting the policy and procedures in writing, we empowered the team to hold each other accountable to the core values of the company in a way that was not based on their opinions or feelings. This is important. The core value policy and procedures create an unbiased third party by which the team can hold each other accountable to the core values in a tactical way in their day-to-day work and interactions.

Core value policy and procedures allow you to get as granular as you like when it comes to the day-to-day policy, procedure, processes, and behaviors in the organization. There are a few other things to keep in mind when you design and create or repurpose your current policy and procedures into core value policy and procedures:

1. You can include products and services in your core value policy and procedures.

---

11 This is a much longer core value policy and procedure. You can view the Inspiring Leadership core value policy and procedures in the appendix of the book.

2. Unlike core value headers or descriptives, you can change your core value policy and procedures when needed.

3. Unlike core value headers or descriptives, core value policy and procedures are not necessarily timeless.

4. Core value policy and procedures can be as long as you like.

5. Core value policy and procedures cannot undermine or contradict your core value header or descriptive.

6. Get creative and make sure your core value policy and procedures are memorable. Our core value policy and procedures were written in the tone and language of the organization.

CONCLUSION

There you have it. These are the key design principles of creating well-designed core values for your organization. I often tell people that well-designed core values take time to build. Just as Steve Jobs spoke about the importance of craftsmanship in building a fence or cabinet, the craftsmanship required in designing core values is the most important aspect to adoption, use, and longevity of these values in any organization. Well-designed core values can become the most potent tool for decision-making and accountability that a company can create—the sky's the limit on the results an organization can experience.

CHAPTER 6

CONGRATS, NOW THE REAL WORK BEGINS— LAUNCHING THE CORE VALUES

Congratulations! You have done some heavy lifting if you followed the steps outlined in the previous chapters and have created a set of core values that follow the principles of this book. Your core values should be authentic to your organization. They should utilize Miller's law so that the end user can easily remember the headers associated with your core value themes. They should have well-designed descriptives that can be used effectively for all decision-making in the organization. They should be built to last a lifetime and beyond. You now have a solid set of core values from which to begin the *real work*. The real work starts with what we call "The Art of the Rollout."

We[12] have designed the art of the rollout in a very specific and strategic way to maximize the effects of launching the core values in the organization. I believe that, when done the right way, this can give an organization's core values rocket-fuel inertia within the organization like you cannot imagine. The rollout has been broken down into five distinct parts that I will be covering in this chapter. Each step is extremely important and needs to be followed exactly as is written in this chapter. I have also included a process for smaller groups, discussed in section six of the chapter.

Warning: This chapter is a step by step guide on how to roll out your core values to your team through a three- to five-hour facilitation. I spared none of the details, giving you the entire process from beginning to end. I want to make sure you get this right in your company. To reiterate what we already stated, this is the most powerful and important part of launching core values in your organization, so skipping this part of the process is not an option. With that said, this chapter is very technical, and most useful when you are getting ready to launch the values in your organization. You can download the complete facilitation and curriculum at www.thecorevalueequation.com/resources.

---

12   I want to acknowledge that there have been some very important people who have been heavily involved in the process of both rolling out the core values and bringing them to life at TMS. Although I have been the architect and leader driving these initiatives, this has been a team effort. I have leaned on many people for their input and effort to create the framework we will be discussing in the next three chapters. Therefore, when appropriate, I will use the word "we" from this point forward when describing our work at TMS.

THE ART OF THE ROLLOUT

1. Prework
   A. Group Dynamics
   B. Working Agreements
2. Me before We
   A. Core Value Reading
   B. Core Value Conversations and Experiences
3. Around the World
4. Me and the Company
5. Ending Strong
   A. HR Paperwork
   B. Warm Thank You
   C. Core Value Celebration
6. Best Practices for Smaller Groups or Solo Hires

The rollout is the most important part of the core value adoption process, after the actual discovery and designing of the core values. Following the process is extremely important. This is where you get the initial momentum behind your core values to help them take hold and come alive in your organization. This is one of the most important moments in an organization regarding the adoption of core values. A good rollout excites the team about the core values, teaches the team the meaning of the core values, and connects the team to the core values.

Earlier, I spoke about the importance of core values being authentic to the personality of the organization. For this to happen, I stated that the team should not be involved in the discovery and design of the core values. Although this may have been true for the *discovery and design* of the core values, it is *not* true for the rollout of the core values. We need their "buy-in." We need the team to understand that this is not just a crazy new idea that the founder and CEO are bringing into the organization from a seminar they went to, which will go away in thirty days. They must understand that this is something more than a "business best practice." It must be communicated that there has been thought and intention given to bringing this into the company. It must be clear that their interests have been considered (even if this means they realize they are not a good fit and should be at another company). This is a big deal for your organization. We need total buy-in. The team's buy-in starts with the proper rollout of the core values.

1. PREWORK

Before we roll out the core values to an organization, we want to be thoughtful about how we introduce them to the existing team. Since there is likely history among team members and between team members and the organization, it is important to curate the rollout and groups with certain dynamics and thoughts in mind. We also want to make sure that the team has all the right expectations regarding how they are to interact with one another during the process of the rollout. I call this part of the rollout "prework." There are two parts to the prework that the management team who rolls out the core values wants to look at and be thoughtful about: group dynamics and working agreements.

a. Group Dynamics

Rolling out the core values to the organization can be a stressful and tedious process. You have likely just spent months discovering, designing, crafting, and building a set of core values that are authentic and true to what the organization stands for. Getting the team to buy into these values can be a complicated and difficult process. You must put the same care and diligence into getting their buy-in as you put into the creation of the core values. The first things to consider are how you want to roll them out to the group and the curation of group dynamics. This will depend greatly on the size of your organization. Here is a rule of thumb: if the organization has less than ten to fifteen people, you should consider doing just one large group rollout. If the organization has more than ten to fifteen people, you should break the group down into groups of eight to ten and do the rollout in smaller groups. The ideal size for this exercise is ten to twelve people per group, and preferably no less than eight. If your organization is smaller than eight people, then do everyone in one group. Size matters because it is hard to moderate groups larger than fifteen people. Groups of eight or fewer are too small, and you don't get a large enough diversity of ideas.

The second thing you want to consider when designing the groups is the current level of trust in the group. The level of trust will dictate how open the team will be in front of the owners, executives, and their managers. Put yourself in the shoes of the secretary of the company. Will they be 100 percent honest about problems they see in the company in front of the CEO? Probably not. It is on you to create a safe environment. In smaller organizations, you will need to use your best judgment regarding designing the groups. In larger companies, the following is the design framework that I recommend:

1. Roll out to C-level and the executive team first
2. Roll out to non-C-level and the non-executive team second

C-Level and Executive Team

In terms of rolling out to the C-level and the executive team first, the idea is that they are the leaders who are taking ownership of what the business looks like on the day-to-day level. This should be the team involved in strategic decision-making in the organization. They should own their respective areas of the company. The other reason you want them segregated is that the non-C-level and non-executive team will open up more if they are doing the exercise separately from the rest of the company. This may not hold true for every organization, but I have found that people tend to be intimidated about being vulnerable, honest, and open in many parts of their life. This exercise asks them to do this in subtle ways. Creating an environment that nurtures their honest thoughts, ideas, and behaviors yields the strongest results as far as buy-in is concerned.

Non–Executive Team

With the non-executive group, especially with larger rollouts (more than three groups), you will want to make sure there are minimal conflicts in the group. For example, you do not want people who manage one another in the same group. You do not want counterparts who may have friction with one another in the same group (think sales management versus back-office management). Think creatively in designing your groups, and try to put people together that have the least involvement with one another within the organization. One of the added benefits of this is that it introduces people who may not otherwise interact. This is especially effective in midsized businesses and larger businesses. Use this as an opportunity to create connectivity for cross-functional relationship building. As you will soon see, the core value rollout forces the team to go deep. This is also a great opportunity for the team to learn about one another. Don't waste this chance to build bridges and bonds all over the organization.

The last thing I like to do is to mix up the group and make it as diverse as possible. You should have all sorts of people, from managers to line-level team members, in the group. This shows that the company is nonhierarchical and that you treat everyone the same. The only exception to this is the C-level and the executive team, which you should group separately. I believe this is a strategic opportunity to get the leadership to buy into this initiative.

b. Working Agreements

Now that you have people broken up into their separate groups, you will want to set aside three to five hours per group to facilitate the entire rollout activity. I recommend not doing more than one group per day. Before you start the core value rollout, you will want to consider doing a working agreement exercise. In my organization, we set up a conference room with a large tripod at the front of the room. Whoever is facilitating asks the group a simple question before we begin:

"In order for us to get the most out of our time together today, what are the expectations we should have for one another?"

Some examples might include the following:

- Turning off cell phones
- No email
- No interrupting one another
- Being respectful
- No talking over each other
- Assuming best intentions
- Honesty
- Being vulnerable when possible

- Being 100 percent present
- Taking breaks

You may want to prompt the team with some of the items I have listed. The goal is to have them come up with what the expectations are. You should write these on a larger Post-it. One of the reasons I like to start with this exercise is because you are sending the message that this is *their* day. This is a nonverbal cue that starts the process of getting their buy-in. If they own the day, then they own the content and the outcome. Once this happens, you have them owning the core values—which is precisely the purpose of the rollout.

I also like to have a special word in the working agreements in the event that someone is breaking the agreement. In my business, we always make this "pepperoni." For instance, let's say someone in the group is not paying attention because they are on their phone, or someone is interrupting, or the entire meeting goes off the rails with people talking over one another. When this happens, anyone in the group can shout, "Pepperoni!" to show the team that the working agreement is being broken. This is a fun and effective way to keep the train on the tracks during meetings like these. It is important to coach the group on this before you get the workshop underway. Once you have the working agreements written on the large Post-it, you should ask everyone in the group to stand up and sign the working agreement. This is important, as it memorializes that this is not just a list of guidelines for the day, but rather a binding social agreement between everyone in the group. Now you are ready to start the workshop.

2. ME BEFORE WE

One of the secrets of getting the buy-in for any movement or cause is to make it personal to the people you are trying to get support from. There is a huge difference between getting people to show up because they feel as if they must be somewhere, and having people show up because they *want* to be there. When rolling out the core values to your team members, it is important to understand the concept of Me before We. The concept of Me before We is that we get the team comfortable with the idea and importance of utilizing core values in a general sense. The mistake that most organizations make is that they ignore the "Me" and focus on the "We." They sit their team down and they force-feed them their core values and culture. This is a mistake. It is a waste of time. If the team member does not buy into the core values of the company and make them their own, then they will not be interested in being part of the team, and at best you will have what I call "words on paper."

Most organizations have words on paper. This is exactly what it sounds like: the founder, CEO, or executive team go on a retreat with some "expert" on culture. They come back with a set of unrelatable, likely bland, non-user-friendly core values. They then drop these core values on the team's lap and hope for the best. Sound familiar? I made this mistake when I launched our core values for the first time at Twin Capital. Remember those disgustingly boring core values?

1. *A positive attitude is imperative for success and growth.*
2. *We treat our customers, coworkers, and business partners with respect and dignity, while maintaining professionalism at all times.*
3. *We believe each individual defines our complete success as a company.*

4. *We value work ethic, ambition, and expertise in our field.*
5. *We strive to retain "A players" and promote from within the company.*
6. *We value proactive behavior that leads to cohesive teamwork in achieving our common objectives.*

Not only were these core values designed poorly, but they were also not relatable. I did not give my team a reason to want to connect with these values. The first step is to focus on the team that you are trying to get buy-in from. This next step is the most important in a core value rollout. Forget, for a second, that you are trying to get someone to believe in *your* cause. This is not about *you*—this has nothing to do with *your* company or organization. You need to focus on what matters most to your team. I will give you a hint: *it is not you.* It has nothing to do with what *you* are trying to build or accomplish. That is a convenient afterthought to your team. What matters to *your* team is the same thing that matters to *you*: they are trying to get what *they* want.

Once you recognize this, you have opened yourself and your organization up to a world of possibility. It is all about *them*. Once you accept that we as people are inherently focused on ourselves, you can then start to strategize to align the needs of the team with the needs of the organization. When these two align, that is when the company can truly try to achieve something special. In the exercise of Me before We, we focus on the team's needs and wants exclusively.

Go back to where we figured out the four to five most important core value themes for the organization. Put the team through this same exercise.

Adventurous	Approachable	Assertive	Caring	Committed	Creative	Authenticity
Courageous	Attentive	Bold	Community	Consistent	Curious	Balance
Energetic	Calm	Collaborative (collaborate)	Compassionate	Dedicated	Innovative	Faith
Enthusiastic	Easy Going	Competent	Conscientious	Dependable	Inventive	Humility
Excellence	Even-tempered	Competitive	Considerate	Disciplined	Talented	Insightful
Freedom	Flexible	Confident	Empathy	Fair	Unique	Intelligent
Inspiring	Great listener	Decisive	Forgiving	Honest		Knowledgeable
Outgoing	Helpful	Determined	Friendly	Integrity		Logical
Passionate	Open-minded	Diligent	Fun-loving	Just		Mindfulness
Risk-taker	Polite	Driven	Generous	Loyal		Modest
Self-made	Prepared	Efficient	Happiness	Responsible		Optimistic
Values-driven	Present	Engaged	Humor	Steadfast		Peaceful
	Responsive	Focused	Kind	Straightforward		Pragmatic
	Service-oriented	Honor	Loving	Trustworthy		Savvy
	Sincere	Independent	Playful			Spiritual
	Thoughtful	Organized	Selfless			Well-rounded
	Tolerant	Positive	Sensitive			Wise
		Proactive				
		Productive				
		Results-oriented				
		Thorough				
		Tradition				

Here is the list of core values. Spend thirty to forty-five minutes to come up with the top five core value themes that are most important to the individual team members in their personal lives. The goal here is for each team member to come up with the core values they themselves live by. After the team comes up with a list, take some time to do the following exercises:

1. Have the team pair off in groups of two to three and ask them to share their number-one core value with their group.
   A. Why did they choose this as their number-one core value?

B. What is their best real-life example of when this core value came to life?

C. Each person should share their partner's number-one core value and story with the group. (15–20 minutes)

2. Have each person share their top five core values with the team. It is important that everyone share, not just volunteers. Go around and look for people who share the same top five core values (e.g., Ryan and Johnny both have the core value of courage in their top five core values). (15–20 minutes)

3. Have members of the team share a moment when their top five core values were challenged.

A. What happened?

B. What did they do to overcome the adversity, utilizing their core values?

C. How did they feel when they were at odds with their core values being challenged? (15–20 minutes)

4. Give each team member a blank sheet of paper. Ask them to design a core value superhero based on one of their top five core values.

A. What is their superpower?

B. What is their weakness?

C. What is their name?

D. What is their superhero symbol?

E. Regardless of artistic ability, have each team member draw a picture of their core value superhero. Go around and have them share what they came up with, with the entire group. (30 minutes)

The goal is to get the team to utilize the language of core values, as it pertains to themselves. It also warms them up to the idea of utilizing core values in their life. You will likely notice a few things in spending this time on your team's personal core values. The team will have fun together, they will learn about each other, they will connect with the importance of having core values, and, most importantly, they will be introduced to the language of core values. You will also see your team loosen up around each other. This is where you want them to be. These exercises get the team warmed up for the teachings that are still to come—the *We* part.

a. Core Value Reading

The next step in the core value rollout is to introduce the core values. This is the unveiling of what you discovered, designed, and created for the organization with the senior leaders of the organization. The core values should be on individual pieces of paper, and each person should have a copy. Ours at TMS look like this:

THE MONEY SOURCE CORE VALUES

People Matter
We take care of our people. Everyone has a voice. At The Money Source, those voices matter. We recognize our workforce by investing in our team members as whole people. We start with making work fun. We weave in a spirit of social responsibility and philanthropy. Over time we build trust and pride. We believe in creating an environment that lends way to our team having fun and engaging in meaningful work. Through this experience we intend to foster a culture of achievement, longevity and excellence.

Inspiring Leadership
Our leaders lead from the front lines and are involved at all levels. While promoting personal accountability and independent thinking, our leadership has the ability to recognize what is needed and is eager to jump in and roll up our sleeves. Our leaders know that leading is about listening and caring for our employees. The satisfaction of our customers is directly related to the happiness of our employees and we work to create positive environments. We believe that actions are the only truth. We strive to be true by consistently modeling and living by The Money Source's vision and creating a culture of high performance, transparency, and accountability.

Strength of Character
We believe that it is integral for each individual to hold one another accountable, regardless of position or rank, to the highest of standards when it comes to the strength of one's character. We recruit team members whose personal values of integrity, work ethic, transparency, and commitment to success as a team match the vision of the organization. Doing right by the organization and our clients is paramount.

Rock Solid Service
The Money Source strives to build a raving fan base through consistent service, quality products and accessibility. We recognize that many team members contribute to our endeavor. Through respect and extraordinary effort, we are able to perform at higher and higher levels. We set ourselves apart from every other organization with our commitment to quality, competence, consistency, and kindness.

Again, the most significant part of the core value rollout is to make it all about the team. I ask for four volunteers who will each read one of the company's core values out loud. This is symbolic. I want the team to take ownership of the core values; this will not happen if I am dictating the core values to them. They need to read the header and descriptive out loud to each other. I like to take a moment between each value to let the core value and the descriptive settle in. Remember: the team member should read *both* the header and the descriptive (although they will not be expected to remember the descriptive, only the header). This is the first step to using the core values in the organization.

Once the core values have been read out loud, I thank the team members and move on to the next step in the process.

b. Core Value Conversations and Experiences

The next step in the process is to have a robust conversation about what core values look like in a company. Remember—at this point, the team has discovered their core values. They have started to use core values in their language, have learned the company's core values, and, lastly, have just read the core values out loud to each other.

Now it's important to get them thinking about the question: *What do core values look like in a business?* I like to ask the team a series of questions, which should promote a robust conversation around what core values look like in a company and their experiences around this idea.

1. How many of you have worked in a company that had core values?

2. What were the core values?
3. Do you remember them?
4. Were they alive and well in those organizations?
5. If yes, how?
6. If no, why not?
7. Did the ownership and C-level consistently live the core values?
8. What do you think about the core values we just read out loud?
9. What thoughts come to mind?

At this point, we don't want to get too far into how the core values will come alive in our organization. The goal here is *context*. We are trying to create context around their past experiences with core values. In my experience, most people will have lukewarm encounters at best. If they are positive, lean into what made them positive. This is less common, though; in general, most companies do not do a very good job of using their core values. The goal is to establish that your organization will be different: you will be more thoughtful and transparent when it comes to having a core-value-driven environment. Having an open discussion with the team about their past experiences sets the stage to do things differently in your organization and takes you one step closer to the team taking ownership of the core values.

3. AROUND THE WORLD

This is probably the most crucial part of the core value rollout. This is an opportunity for the team to have a robust discussion and ideation regarding what the core values will look like if they are alive and well in the company. It is also an opportunity to discuss what the core values will look like if they are *not* alive and well in the company. These are the directions to begin the exercise:

1. Write each core value on a large Post-it.
2. Put the large Post-its along opposing walls. Make sure there is enough space so that a group of four to five people can stand in front of their Post-it without being on top of one another, and so that they are not interrupting the other groups.
3. Break the team up into groups of three to five people. The ideal size is four people. The maximum size of each rollout group is sixteen people, so you will need to play with the number based on the size of the overall training group and how many core values you have.
4. Once the team is broken up into smaller groups, I assign a core value to each group as a starting point for the exercise.

Let's use TMS's core values to illustrate.

- People Matter.
- Inspiring Leadership
- Strength of Character
- Rock Solid Service

Let's use a training group of sixteen to illustrate:

1. Break the group up into teams of four people. You will now have four groups of four.
2. Have each group stand in front of one of the four core values.
3. Have each group grab a different colored marker. (this is a key part of the exercise; make sure the groups do not have the same color of marker)

I then give them the following instructions:

1. Take three minutes to write down any word, action, or example of what would need to be true in our company for the core value you are standing in front of to be alive and well in the organization.
   A. What are examples of what the core value would look like in action?
   B. What word/words do you associate with the core value?
   C. What feelings?
   D. How is the company currently living the core value you are standing in front of?
   E. How can the company expand on this and make it even better?
2. After three minutes, move clockwise to the next core value. Ignore anything the other group(s) have written. It is completely okay for the groups to have overlapping or similar words and ideas.
3. The moderator will need to reset the clock each time the three-minute marker is hit and provide thirty seconds to get to the next core value. I like to yell, "Time!" when the three minutes are up, then "Switch!" so that the groups know to move to the next core value.
4. Once each group has had a chance to ideate in front of each core value, I ask them to stay standing in front of the core value they just finished working on.
5. I then give them the following instructions: "The next phase of the core value exercise is to look at what each group has written."
   A. What stands out to you?
   B. Where is there commonality and overlap?
   C. Underline, in your colored marker, areas of overlap, redundancy, and the most important ideas and themes

that you truly believe stand out for this core value to be alive and well in our organization. This can be anything on the Post-it, not just what your team wrote.

I then give them one minute per core value for this exercise. After I call time, I instruct them to move to the next core value.

6. Each team should be identifying the most important themes, ideas, and areas of overlap between the groups. When sixty seconds pass, I call, "Time!" and then shout, "Switch!" Each team has fifteen to thirty seconds to move to the next core value. Remember, this should be a quick exercise.

7. Once each team has had a chance to do each core value, I call final time. I ask them to stay standing in front of the core value they ended on. I then ask each team to pick a team captain to represent them to the entire group for the next part of the exercise.

8. This is an opportunity to have an open discussion about what they found and what stood out to them regarding the core value they are standing in front of. The team captain presents the areas that the team seemed to agree on most. After the team representing the core value has presented, the discussion is opened up to the entire group for feedback. We do this for each core value in order, from the first group to the last group.

9. At this point, the team has spent twenty to thirty minutes talking about what needs to happen for the core values to be alive and well in the organization. They have spoken about what currently exists and what may need to change. The creative juices should be flowing. The group should feel as though they have a voice in the direction the organization takes, and that they are a collective group agreeing on these ideas. They should be in a very good place for the next step.

10. People should now remain with their teams and sit down. There should be a robust group discussion about the entire exercise.

   A. What stood out to them?

   B. What are some examples of how the company currently lives the core values that they would like to share?

   C. What are some areas we might want to consider for improvement?

   D. What are some areas that might be a challenge to one or all of these core values continuing to be believed as true in the organization going forward?

   E. What are some challenges that could derail the core values that we may want to be proactive about protecting?

The goal in this group discussion is for the team to be heard. When done correctly, the team should have been able to exhaust their thoughts on what the core values will look like in the organization. *This is one of the most powerful and important exercises regarding the rollout and birth of the core values.* It is a symbol of the company's commitment to these values. The fact that the company would spend so much time, energy, and thought allowing the team to connect with core values truly sets the tone. Once this happens, the team takes ownership of what the future of these values will look like in the organization. With this exercise, conversation, and activity, the company is put on the strongest path to successfully building a core-value-driven organization.

4. ME AND THE COMPANY

At this point in the core value facilitation, you should have a team of people who understand their personal core values and what the company's core values stand for. They have spent three to four hours talking and working with the idea of core values and what they look like in the world around them. This is a fantastic position to be in for the next activity of the day, known as "Me and the Company." This is where we connect the dots. We will now connect the team member's personal core values with the company's core values. This is not just about the team member's needs, nor is it just about the company's needs. It's about how each set of needs comes together to represent one united front to the world. The instructions for this exercise are as follows:

1. Get four to five (depending on how many core value themes you end up with) large poster-sized Post-its and write a core value header on each of them.
2. Below each core value, have each team member write down any of their personal, top-five core values that they believe are represented in or aligned with the specific company core value header.
    A. Participants can have more than one personal core value under each of the company's core values, and they can use the same personal core value more than once if it connects.
    B. Participants should also, on a separate sheet of paper, write down why each specific personal core value relates to the company core value they are attaching it to.

For example:

My personal core values are:

- Love
- Creativity
- Courage

- Mindfulness
- Knowledge

I then look at each company core value and see which of my personal core values relate to a specified company core value. Let's start by looking at "People Matter."

People Matter.

We take care of our people. Everyone has a voice. At TMS, those voices matter. We recognize our workforce by investing in our team members as whole people. We start by making work fun. We weave in a spirit of social responsibility and philanthropy. Over time, we build trust and pride. We believe in creating an environment that allows our team to have fun and engage in meaningful work. Through this experience, we intend to foster a culture of achievement, longevity, and excellence.

Four of my five personal core values connect with "People Matter." for the following reasons:

- Love
- Creativity
- Courage
- Mindfulness

Love

By creating an environment where we show love toward our team, we show our team that they are important to us. We do this by making work fun and creating an environment where our people have a voice. By caring for our team, we represent this core value and show our team that they are very important to us.

Creativity

We are always changing it up. We are creative in our team builds to create a fun environment, and we think outside the box on ways to help our team be engaged and feel as though they have a voice in our organization.

Courage

We show our courage by doing the right thing for our team even when it is not easy. The idea around this is that we put the people first, not the person first. Every decision we make is for the greater good of the organization and, sometimes, that may not be aligned with one or two specific individuals.

Mindfulness

We have a consciousness around our people. We are aware that this is their livelihood and that we must show respect for them and their families. We are aware that, in the world of business, it can be challenging to build trust with a team. Many of our people may have worked in organizations that did not exhibit mindfulness about their people. We are different and need to show this with our actions.

I usually give the team around thirty minutes to go around the room and connect their personal values with the company core values. The expectation is that they put their name and the specific core value(s) on the different core value Post-its. On a separate worksheet (you can find this worksheet at www.thecorevalueequation.com/resources), they list the core value and the reason why their personal core value connects with the company core value.

After the team has had time to do this, have them circle up and have a group discussion to go over what was found. I engage participants in a nice discussion asking the following questions:

1. What did you find?
2. Which of your core values really connected well with the company core values?
3. Why?
4. What else did you notice?
5. Was there overlap (i.e., one core value connected with many or all of the company core values)?

What you will find is that there are many different experiences regarding connection. We also find that there is a lot of overlap. Many of the team members' personal core values align to many of the company core values. It is a powerful and great representation that our team's core values are aligned well with our company core values. Inversely, sometimes there are gaps and core value misalignment. There is nothing wrong with this—it is a nice representation of authenticity on the part of the company and the team members. The team truly gets to see just how aligned they are with the company. The goal is to attract talent whose core values align with the company values and for participants who don't align to self-select out of the organization.

5. ENDING STRONG

By the time that you reach this part of the core value rollout, you have likely spent four to five hours diving very deep with the team. You have shared personal stories and talked about the company in a real and honest way. You should have allowed your team to have a voice in shaping the future of the organization. You will have their buy-in and their attention. Your team will be exhausted. It is likely that the team has never had an experience like this at a company they have worked at before. This is the type of feedback we have consistently received at TMS from our team over the past six years. Given how powerful the day has already been, it is extremely important that you end the day strong. I recommend a couple of easy things you can do to help guarantee an effective ending to the day.

a. HR Paperwork

We always start with core value onboarding with our new hires and end with human resources paperwork. We have found that new team members really appreciate this. It shows that we recognize our team as "people" first and "paperwork" second. We have received countless compliments over the years, and I highly recommend you do this in your organization. Paperwork should only be given to the participants after the entire facilitation is completed.

b. Warm Thank You

After we wrap up the Me and the Company part of the rollout facilitation, we always express our immense gratitude to the team for their contribution to the day. We communicate how excited we are to bring these core values to life in the coming weeks, months, and years in our organization. I always end with the following exercise:

1. I personally like to have everyone stand in a circle and hold hands with the person on each side.
2. Once everyone is holding hands, I take a second to let the connectivity set in.
3. I then look everyone in the eyes and give them a warm *thank*

you for the privilege of spending time with them. I thank them for taking the time to be a part of our company's future. Lastly, I thank them for the effort that they have and will give in the future in creating a core-value-driven organization.

I also include that our journey is not a perfect road. Your team should understand that the core values shine the brightest when things are tough and when things don't go our way. It's important to set the expectation that the core values are not perfection. Core values are not a utopia where everyone will automatically live the core values every day. It is never sunshine and rainbows from here to eternity. Core values are a benchmark to return to. The only way they come to life is when the team—not just the leadership—believes in and holds one another accountable for living the core values. When this happens, the core values have a chance of becoming the standard for behavior in the organization.

I always end a rollout session by saying the following:

"Nothing warms my heart more than when I hear one of two things uttered by my team:

"'Hey, thank you [insert team member's name]—you really lived [insert appropriate core value header]. I really appreciate that you did [insert behavior that connects to specific core value]!' or

"'Hey, [insert team member's name]—you are not living [insert appropriate core value header]. I really don't appreciate that you did [insert behavior that connects to specific core value]!'"

The team members recognizing one another is a win for the company. This shows the core values are being used as a standard for behavior and are part of the language of the organization. I would rather team members praise each other for following core values than point out that the others are not adhering to them, but both illustrate the team is engaging in using the core values and holding each other accountable for living up to the standard. This is also very important since it demonstrates that the team is using the core values as the language of accountability within the organization.

c. Core Value Celebration

Congratulations to you and your team. You have done it! You have officially launched the core values in your organization. The next step is celebrating. Go get pizza, grab some beers, host a team build. Make sure the event involves lots of socializing, and make sure it occurs within one hour of finishing the workshop. This is a crucial part of the launch. It allows the team a moment to decompress, rub elbows, have fun, and build trust. It shows the team that this is an important part of the company, and that you appreciate them taking the time to contribute and be part of something greater than themselves.

6. BEST PRACTICES FOR SMALLER GROUPS OR SOLO HIRES

The onboarding outlined in this chapter includes the best practices for rolling out the core values in groups of eight or more. It is possible to have one group as small as three or four people. Any smaller than three people and you will want to use the workbook I have designed for introducing your core values to your team. You can download the workbook at www.thecorevalueequation.com/resources. The workbook is called *Individual Core Value Onboarding Workbook*. The workbook is designed to have one seasoned person from your team sit down with the new hire and spend a couple of hours going through the workbook exercises and results with the new team member. It is best to use the workbook when you are only onboarding one or two people at a time. The workbook covers the activities I outlined in this chapter:

1. Me before We
2. Core Value Reading
3. Core Value Conversations and Experiences
4. Around the World
5. Me and the Company

These are the five most important areas of the workshop that can be converted into an individual or small-group activity. The point of the activity is still the same; however, the onboarding method is executed differently.

CONCLUSION

You should now have a strong roadmap of how to initially introduce new and existing team members to your core values. Pat yourself on the back—this is a large milestone and you have a great deal to be excited about! The next chapter will look at practical and tactical ways to keep this core value rocket ship in orbit after launch.

CHAPTER 7

HOW TO MAKE YOUR CORE VALUES STICKY

Let's be clear: core values are not a static element in your company. They are not something you put out into the world once and then expect to take hold in an organization. Your core values are a set of standards to which you hold everyone accountable within the company. If these values are firmly established, then you and your team relate to them and they become the standard by which your customers can hold your company accountable. In other words, if the core values are alive and well, then your customers' experience should mirror what is happening within the organization—they should be experiencing what you say your core values are.

Core values are like a marriage. In a marriage, you can't just go on one date a year and expect to have a great relationship. In a marriage, you can't expect to have a great wedding and then ignore your spouse and assume your marriage will flourish. As in any relationship, it takes work to make the partnership thrive. All too often, organizations have their core value wedding—in other words, they roll out the core values to their teams—and then they think the work is done. If you plan on doing this, you will not build a core-value-driven organization. There is a very low likelihood that the core values will be alive, well, and consistent within the organization. Core values need to become the oxygen in the air of the organization. No single act will accomplish this. It requires many small, easy, user-friendly acts to ensure those values stay alive and well.

When we see the core values as a relationship rather than a static element, this changes how we bring them to life in the organization. The goal is for the core values to become the language of the organization. When we learn a foreign language, we don't start by reading a four-hundred-page novel. We start with the simplest forms of the language and then grow from there. The same is true with bringing the core values to life in a company. We start by choosing a few small acts and activities and then, once they become commonplace, we add another. And another. And then another. It is not one small or large act that counts; rather, it is dozens of small acts that will make the core values come alive in the organization. Before you know it, the core values are everywhere. They become known and are widely used in the company. I call this making the core values *sticky*.

There is a quote that I love by Starbucks' Howard Schultz. Someone had allegedly asked Schultz, "Howard, what is it? What is it that makes Starbucks so successful? Is it the Italian lounge-y feel? Is it the way you guys call a medium a grande? Is it the music in the stores? Is it the pastries you guys serve? What is it? What is it that makes Starbucks…Starbucks?"

Howard Schultz said, "It's everything. It's a thousand little things. That's what makes us successful."

I truly believe that to make core values sticky in an organization, you must have this perspective. It's not going to be one thing that makes them come to life in the organization; there are a lot of little things that need to happen consistently.

This chapter is a guide to bringing the core values to life in a sticky and user-friendly way. The aim here is to make the process easy and user-friendly so that the core values are accessible and can be used in a consistent manner. I often see organizations start this process very gung ho. Leaders exert a massive amount of energy and enthusiasm around launching core values into their organization, only to fall flat on their face when they get busy and go back to business as usual. This is a mistake. I have found, over the last thirteen years of experimenting with bringing core values to life, that, as with Starbucks, it's doing the important little things consistently that yields the greatest results. This idea around creating lasting change is best explained in the work of psychologist B.J. Fogg, in his book *Tiny Habits: The Small Changes That Change Everything*. Fogg was interviewed by NPR regarding the ideas presented in his book:

> According to B.J. Fogg, a psychologist and researcher at Stanford University who has studied behavior change for more than 20 years, doing something you don't enjoy and subsequently failing to make it habitual is actually more detrimental to a mission for change than doing nothing at all. To create a real lifelong habit, the focus should be on training your brain to succeed at small adjustments, then gaining confidence from that success, he argues. To do that, one needs to design behavior changes that are both

easy to do and can be seamlessly slipped into your existing routine. Aim for automaticity.[13]

To help people figure out how to make new behaviors they actually want as routine as turning to Google to search the web, he developed the Fogg Method, which references several psychological theories and is comprised of three key steps. The first is about identifying your specific desired outcome: Do you want to feel less stressed at work? Lose 10% of your body weight? Next, identify the easy-win behaviors—he calls them "tiny habits"—that will put you on the path to that goal. Finally, find a trigger—something that you already do as a habit—and graft the new habit onto it. That might mean putting out an apple on the counter every time you start the coffeemaker in the morning," Fogg explained to NPR. "Notice I didn't say eat the apple," he added.[14]

The desired outcome we are looking for is to get the team to remember the core values and to use the core values in their daily work routine. This helps team members manage themselves and their team members to an expected and desired outcome when it comes to behavior in the workplace. We will explore five areas in which you can make small and sustainable changes in your organization that will make the core values commonplace. Your core values will become "the oxygen in the air" of your organization. We use some of the methods described by Fogg to help bring the core values to life. The key here is to start small, make them a habit, add another, then another, and so on. The following ideas should be done in order.

---

13   Lila MacLellan, "A Stanford University Psychologist's Elegant Three-Step Method for Creating New Habits," *Quartz*, January 4, 2017, https://qz.com/877795/how-to-create-new-good-habits-according-to-stanford-psychologist-b-j-fogg/.

14   Take Care Staff, "How to Make Healthy Life Changes from Tiny Habits," WRVO, August 13, 2006, https://www.wrvo.org/post/how-make-healthy-life-changes-tiny-habits.

HOW TO CREATE STICKY CORE VALUES

1. Core Value Advertising
2. Core Value Storytelling
3. Core Value Recruiting and Hiring
4. Bleeding Core Values
   A. Core Value Mascot
   B. Core Value Symbols
   C. Core Value Swag
5. Core Value Communications and Awards

1. CORE VALUE ADVERTISING

Just as companies use advertising to promote their products and services, I believe that advertising our core values is extremely important when making the core values come to life in any organization. The first thing you need to do once your core values are built is put them out so that the team and customers can see them easily. Core values should be as visible as possible in areas that get high foot traffic. I recommend two obvious spots: your brick-and-mortar and virtual walls.

The idea is to not be shy about your core values. I like to pick high-traffic areas in my office spaces and make these values as visible as possible. As illustrated earlier, I usually display the core value header along with the core value descriptive. I also like to pick the biggest wall in the space with the most visibility and traffic, and strategically place the values in that location. This is a crucial statement: it is a subtle way to get the core values out in front of the team. My business is mostly B2B, but if you are consumer-facing, then displaying them is even more important because it shows your customers that you are a core-value-driven organization.

The same is true for your team. Displaying the core values makes the statement loud and clear that this is how you are leading the company. To display wall signage that is ten feet to fifteen feet long and ten feet to fifteen feet tall in a high-traffic area makes a very clear statement to your team. It becomes a monument to your organization's commitment to the core values. If you have a large office, then you may want to have more than one of these signs. I would say one per one hundred employees. If you have a space with five hundred employees, you may want to replicate this in five locations so that it gets seen. I also say about one per ten thousand square feet. The point is that you want these values visible and seen. Wall signage is an easy and efficient way to spread the message in a powerful and passive way.

Here is an example of our core value wall that we have posted in our TMS Phoenix, AZ, office.

The same idea is true about having your core values on your website. This is another way to say, "We are a core-value-driven organization—here are our values, this is what they mean to us, and you should expect the following when you do business with us." This is yet another subtle and bold way to show everyone what the organization stands for.

I also recommend making core value posters. You can get very creative with this. We show the core values *with* their descriptives and we treat them like moveable artwork—they are framed and hung all over the place.

The goal is to create a passive visual connection to the team, both in the real world and digitally. It makes the core values a permanent fixture in the company for everyone to see. Don't be shy about your core values. It was a ton of work to build them. This is your first foray into using and teaching the team the core values post-rollout. Have fun—put them everywhere!

Image of our core value signage with a team member at our Melville, NY, office

Image of our core value signage with a team member at our Meriden, CT, office

Image of our core value signage in a TMS office

Image of our core values posted on the TMS website

Image of our first core value wall in a TMS office

2. CORE VALUE STORYTELLING

Core value storytelling is probably the most powerful and underrated method of bringing core values to life in the organization. Humans learn best through stories, plain and simple. Stories allow audiences to process and retain information because they evoke our emotions. Research shows that 70 percent of what we learn is consumed through storytelling.[15]

One of the easiest and most powerful ways in which we have integrated our core values into TMS is through the use of storytelling. I recommend using one of the following:

1. Weekly or biweekly survey
2. Internal communication tool: 15Five, CultureIQ, TINYPulse, Culture Amp, SurveyMonkey

In our company, we have an internal system for surveying that we call "Pink Pulse." We survey our team to gather feedback on a regular basis. We do this every other week, which is a routine that works well for us. The first question we ask in our survey is the following:

Can you tell us an example or story about one of our team members who lived one of our core values this week? What is their name? Which core value did they live? How did they live the core value?

We get hundreds of stories of our team living the core values. We then take all the responses and publish them to the entire organization.

---

15 "Hardwired to Learn through Story," Story Preservation Initiative, November 1, 2012, https://storypreservation.wordpress.com/2012/11/01/hardwired-to-learn-through-story/.

Pink Pulse 11/4/2019

1. Which Core Value(s) did you see someone live this week? Can you tell us in detail the story behind how they lived the core value? (required)

2. How are you feeling? What is the morale you see around you? (required)

3. What do you need help with? This week? This month? (required)

4. During the past year, which part(s) of your work gave you the most satisfaction? What have you found challenging? (required)

Opt Out   Cancel   Save as Draft   Complete

Here is an example of the pink pulse survey we send out to our team on a biweekly basis at TMS.

NAME	ANSWERS
Frank Connor	**Brand Bentley** shows Rock Solid Service all the time. He handles all calls as if their his own files and makes sure to thoroughly explain what is going on with a file
Brandon Vickers	Our new lead **Luke Knight** has been very active with updates and taking escalated calls. She is doing a great job!!
Christy Anderson	**Jenny Salter** assisted with assigning loans while I was out, she did great and exemplified Rock Solid Service!
Brand Bentley	**Chad Peppers** He lives all the Core Values! He truly is a leader and always goes above and beyond for anyone and everyone at TMS. He has a kind heart and goes out of his way to bring a smile to everyone's face. We are lucky to have him!
Erica Black	**Justice Warran**, always a joy to work with on the many projects going on. She approached various initiatives and projects with a motivated GSD attitude. Rock Solid Service!

Above is an example of entries we received for our core value question that we ask our team. Question response rate: 180 out of 375 participants (48.00 %).

This is one of my favorite methods to bring the core values to life for a few reasons.

1. The team must actively think of someone who lived the core values. But to do that, *they need to know what the core values are.* This forces them to think critically about the core values and then put them in context in a way that tells a story.

2. The team is now giving each other recognition, using the core values as the standard by which they are both giving and receiving an acknowledgment. This puts the core values on a pedestal. It elevates the importance of the core values within the company.

3. When the company publishes this to the team, it shows, once again, that these core values are important and that they are the standard that we use to drive behavior in the organization. This shows our team that the core values are being used all throughout the organization and it gives the team permission to start using them in a positive way.

The hundreds of stories we get also give us a springboard to see what people are doing in the company. We get to see peer-to-peer acknowledgment, and this uncovers core-value-driven acts that perhaps would not have been noticed had we not made this something we consistently do. My company has been doing this for six years, and we now have tens of thousands of core value stories that have been told at TMS. Nothing makes me prouder than reading individual acts of living the core values, and I get the honor of doing this every two weeks. This is an easy and user-friendly way to publish core-value-driven stories to your entire organization.

If I were to offer three key takeaways from this book after creating your core values, they would be the following:

1. Roll out the core values to the team using the engaging and meaningful process outlined in chapter 6.

2. Display the core values on your walls—in your offices and on your website.
3. Ask your team which team members lived the core values every week/every other week, and share the stories with your company.

The next items I will cover are great to add, but these three actions will get you very far in making the core values come to life in your organization—and they are extremely easy to do.

3. CORE VALUE RECRUITING AND HIRING

Another easy way to push the core values to the outside world is through the recruiting and hiring process. Core values act as a filter for the organization's recruiting process. The core values will allow the organization to attract talent who share the organization's core beliefs and values. The core values should also block those who are not a fit from joining your organization. Remember when Brian told me "that's not my job" back at Twin Capital Mortgage? He was not a core value fit. Had I had the core value of "Do Work!" in place when he was in our hiring process, there would have been a much lower chance he would have found his way into our company. Integrating core values into your recruiting and hiring process is low-hanging fruit for making the core values come alive in your organization.

There are a few best practices that I have integrated into our organizations over the years that have served us well.

1. **Use the web**: I already discussed having your core values on your website. When a candidate is researching your company, they will likely come upon these values. This allows you to check whether they did any homework on your

company before applying for a position. You don't know how many times I have had a candidate comment, "Wow, you guys are really all about your core values! I saw them on your website and all over the web." This is not the sole reason to have them on your website, of course; however, it sends a message that this is important to the organization, which helps to attract the right type of team members and customers. This outcome creates a stronger company, as you begin to have better alignment throughout the company around the leadership's beliefs and build a raving fanbase.

2. **Include them in your job posting**: Like having the core values on your website, I often recommend posting your core values first and foremost in your job postings. I recommend doing this before you describe the job and job duties. This is a trust marker. It shows the world that the core values are the most important thing that the company stands for. I often add something to the posting along the lines of "If you share in our core values, then we encourage you to continue reading this posting as you may have found a great home for your career." Leading with the core values in the job posting shows what is important to the organization.

3. **Conduct a core value interview**: Once core values are in the job posting, it is only natural to incorporate the core values into the interview process. I recommend designing job interview questions around the core values. At TMS, we ask our candidates the following questions:

   A. Our number-one core value is "People Matter." Provide an example of a time when you demonstrated this core value in your personal and professional life. Can you tell me about a time when you might have broken this core value in your personal life or professional life?

   B. Our number-two core value is "Strength of Character." Provide an example of a time when you demonstrated this core value in your personal and professional life. Can you tell me about a time when you might have broken this core value in your personal life or professional life?

The goal here is to dig into our core values and see if the person is a core value fit for the organization. This is not to say we don't ask other questions about their relevant work experience and/or other hiring best practices. We do, however, lead with our core values and make sure it is a part of the language used when determining if the person is a good fit for our culture and team. Another added benefit to this is the core value journey it creates for the prospective team member. Allow me to explain. The first thing the candidate sees is our core values in the job posting. They will then likely research our company and find our core values on our website and online. We then lead with the core values in the hiring process. If they are hired, their first experience of being onboarded in our company is a day of learning about *their* core values, the company core values, and how they relate to one another. If this is not a statement to the prospective recruit about what the company stands for, then I do not know what is. Think of how this might differ from how you are currently recruiting and hiring candidates. What kind of talent is *not* joining your company because of your current hiring process? We have found that, by building our hiring process and connecting it to our onboarding, we have a filter that is attracting top talent with amazing alignment to our core values, as well as dissuading potential misfits.

4. BLEEDING CORE VALUES

One of my favorite exercises when teaching team members about core values is to ask them a simple question: "Think back to when you were ten years old. How many of you dreamed about being in the mortgage industry?" (I say the mortgage industry because that's our field, but change it according to your industry.) I always get a smile from the group. I then ask them to raise their hands if this was their childhood dream. Ninety-nine percent of the time, it is not the dream of a ten-year-old to be in the mortgage industry. The 1 percent of the time that people say they dreamed about being in the industry is when one of their parents was in the industry and they wanted to be just like their mom or dad.

"Wait, so none of you dreamed about being a loan processor or loan officer? You didn't hope and wish to be in the mortgage business when you were in fourth or fifth grade?" I ask in mock surprise. "Well then, when you were ten, what did you want to be when you grew up?"

I love to hear the array of answers that I get from people:

- Lawyer
- Doctor
- Professional actor/actress
- Professional singer
- Bull rider
- Teacher
- Banker
- Professional football player
- Professional baseball player
- Professional soccer player
- Professional basketball player
- The president of the United States
- Astronaut
- Chef

These are a few of the more popular answers I have received over the years. People rarely end up in the dream job they imagined when everything and anything was possible. The fact is, very few people end up in the job or industry that they dreamed of when they were a child.

"Look, none of you dreamed about being in the mortgage industry, myself included. But here we all are. We have two choices. One, we can treat this like a job and show up and grind through our days, weeks, months, and years to make a paycheck. Or, two, we can be a part of something greater than ourselves. The only way I know of doing this is by making this business about something more than any one of us. We can bring our core values to life and build a core-value-driven environment. From that, we can strive to build a world-class organization."

When I say these words to my team, I always notice the subtle movement of their heads, nodding "yes." We all strive to live a life of purpose. It is wired into our DNA. Your teams are striving to find purpose in their lives and jobs as well. If you are a doctor or a nurse, maybe this is easier to find. But what about if you own a janitorial company? What if you process loan applications? What if you work at the DMV? We can find purpose in anything. Core values offer a language and opportunity to bring a higher meaning to one's organization.

Another example of this is professional sports teams. I'd always notice many of our staff members obsessing about their sports teams in the San Francisco Bay Area. I would often hear conversations on Monday morning about how the Raiders had played, or the 49ers, Giants, Oakland A's, Golden State Warriors, or San Jose Sharks. Many of the folks having these conversations were in positions ranging from an entry-level loan administrator to an executive vice president. I saw that this was a great representation of people believing in something greater than themselves. In this instance, it was a local professional sports team.

When I was sixteen years old, I had the amazing opportunity of being the class president of my high school. During this experience, I was constantly involved in promoting school spirit during our pep rallies, school dances, sporting events, and so on. In fact, I was voted "most spirited" in my senior class (Go Canyon Commanches!). As a CEO, I used my observation of professional sports teams and high school spirit as examples of people getting behind something larger than themselves. The following are activities, initiatives, and items we have rolled out in our company to help our team bleed our core values. They are quite simple and easy to implement and, when done well, are an amazing way to bring the core values to life in any organization.

A. CORE VALUE MASCOT

College teams, high school teams, and professional teams are great examples of organizations that utilize a mascot to help rally their people around a third-party symbol for what those organizations stand for. At TMS, our mascot is a pink unicorn. Why a pink unicorn? A pink unicorn symbolizes happiness in the mortgage industry. The happiness is brought to life by our company being a core-value-driven organization. Pink unicorns and mortgages? Seems crazy, right? Maybe so, but, at TMS, our team is obsessed with pink unicorns (see pictures). By having a mascot, our core values are brought to life in a tangible way. This gives us tools to support the core values within the organization in a more playful and exciting way. It also attracts people to our company who are attracted to what we stand for. The goal here is to give the team tools to bring the core values to life. We have found that by making the core values fun and exciting, we can get the team more engaged in using these values.

This is what we call the pink unicorn pose.

Pink Unicorn Lounge in our Melville, NY, office

A team member wearing a pink unicorn onesie at one of our offices

My old LinkedIn profile page. This is what I call a pink unicorn Superman pose!

Yes, this is actually our tradeshow booth. You can say we don't like to hide our true colors!

When someone gives you a pink unicorn mask as a gift, you need to show it off!

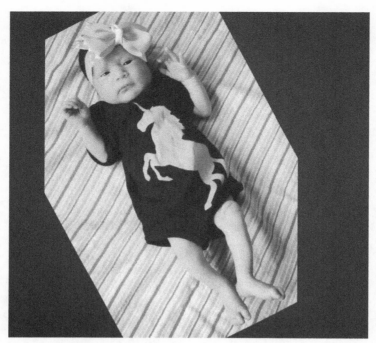

All of our newborns get their very own pink unicorn baby onesie.

My son Pablo as a baby rocking a pink unicorn T-shirt

B. CORE VALUE SYMBOLS

As we did with the mascot, we designed core value symbols to support what the core values mean. This simplifies the values and makes them accessible. At TMS we developed the following four symbols for our core values:

Here's why we decided on the following designs for our core value symbols at TMS:

People Matter.

The lightbulbs with heart-shaped filaments stand for the people in our company. This shows that we care about their hearts and their minds. It also shows that we value them as people and we value their opinions.

Inspiring Leadership

We used the image of a torch to symbolize the idea of leading the way. The fire burning in the torch represents being inspirational and passionate leaders to our people and to those around us.

Strength of Character

For this core value symbol, we chose a sailor's knot to symbolize doing the right thing for our organization. This is a bit of an analogy, but the idea is that where there is integrity, there is strength. The knot represents the strength that we have in our organization when we deliver on our promise of having a company that has unquestionable integrity.

Rock Solid Service

There are two parts to this symbol. The first is a mountain. We used El Capitan from Yosemite National Park to show a strong granite mountain. This supports the rock portion of the core value. The flag on top of the mountain symbolizes greatness and giving amazing service.

To understand the power of symbols, you must understand why symbols were created in the first place. For the first 470,000 years of human communication, people used speech. Things were remembered and passed down, but not recorded. As soon as someone stopped talking, the only reliable record of that information was in the memory of the listener. With the advent of symbols, the intended meanings of ideas, concepts, and thoughts were able to be captured and accessible to those who were not around to hear the original communication.

Symbols represented a new way to record information and increase the longevity of ideas, concepts, and thoughts. Think of symbols as a way to build longevity in your core values. Word of mouth will rise and fall from day to day, but symbols are a much more digestible representation of a brand that is built to last.

When developing a core value symbol, do not build on a passing industry fad or a temporary trend. Create a core value symbol that's timeless.

This is a perfect example of bringing the core values to life in a new and inventive way. Treat each symbol as a core value logo.

This does a few things. First, it gives your team a visual cue by which they can remember the core value. It also helps tell the story of the core value, reinforcing the goal of making these values memorable. Second, symbols give the organization collateral that can be used to promote the core values in the organization. These symbols can be displayed on signage, posters, websites, bags, T-shirts, polos, and so on. Symbols become a fun, inventive, and memorable way to bring the core values to life in the organization.

C. CORE VALUE SWAG

Once you have developed an array of core value collateral (e.g., core value symbols, a mascot, and so on), it's time to have fun with these items and put them to use. When I was my high school class president, there was a school store that sold T-shirts, baseball caps, beanies, sweatshirts, hoodies, posters, socks, ribbons, coffee mugs, and more. These items were adorned with our high school mascot and colors. Many colleges and universities have these items to promote school spirit. When you go to professional sports events, they sell an array of items promoting their teams in this same way. At TMS, we have done the same thing with our company mascot, colors, and core value symbols. The idea is to create an army of supporters who proudly wear the company swag. Here are some ideas to promote these items inside and outside your organization that will give you a sense of how we have done this at TMS:

- Quarterly themed T-shirts
- Pink unicorn T-shirt
- Core value logo T-shirt
- Folders with the company core value symbols on the cover
- Notebooks with the company core values on the cover
- Shoelaces with the company core values on them
- Pink unicorn blanket

- Pink unicorn onesie (yes, we really have this)
- Beanies promoting the core values and the pink unicorn
- Polo shirt with a pink unicorn on the chest (think Lacoste shirt)
- Jackets, backpacks, sweatshirts, computer bags—all with the core value symbols and/or the pink unicorn printed
- Water bottles, coffee mugs, flasks, stickers, iron-ons, umbrellas—you name it, we print our mascot and core values on it, and sell it or people can earn it at our company store.

The idea is to make these symbols omnipresent. By promoting these symbols in the same way your favorite sports team promotes their team gear, we create a sense of belonging in our team. This is how professional/college/high school sports teams represent their team spirit. Like a sports team and its fans, the company team is now part of something greater than themselves. At TMS, our offices and people have become physical manifestations of our culture through the use of all these items. Everywhere you look, you see our core values, whether it be on the walls, signage, or gear.

We have also done two other things to help promote our gear in the company to support the mascot and core values. We have devoted two days a week to wearing these items:

TMS Tuesdays—Every Tuesday, we encourage our teams to wear TMS gear. This can be any of the items I mentioned above. The idea is to make this fun and casual. Like many work environments that are business casual, we make this day a jeans and T-shirt day. You can wear casual clothes if you wear company swag. If not, then you need to dress in business casual attire (this can be business attire, depending on your company's dress code). The idea is to reward the team for supporting the company.

TMS Tuesday in our Melville, NY, office

TMS Tuesday in our Phoenix, AZ, office

TMS Tuesday pic in front of pink unicorn signage

TMS Tuesday with the team enjoying some unicorn cereal

TMS Tuesday in our Concord, CA, office

TMS Tuesday in our Meriden, CT, office

Tracksuit Thursdays—This started as something fun we did early on. We would all wear tracksuits (think Run DMC and disco tracksuits), have a dance competition, and give away prizes to the winner. This transformed into pink unicorn tracksuits, whereby team members could earn an Adidas tracksuit with the company logo and pink unicorn embroidered on the jacket.

We created strict criteria to qualify for earning one of these pink unicorn tracksuits. We took the idea of the letterman jacket and made it into something we could use to promote those who live our core values. By making the tracksuit an exclusive item, we then promote the idea that those who wear it have achieved an advanced and proven level of living our core values. This is probably one of the most popular things we have done at TMS. Every Thursday, these tracksuits are proudly worn by all those who have earned them by living the core values. It is such a hit that we have had many people outside our organization ask if they could buy a pink unicorn tracksuit. Unfortunately, not all things are for sale. In our company, those who have proven they live the core values earn their tracksuit. We devote one day per week for hundreds of our teammates, whom we call pink unicorns, to proudly wear these tracksuits to show the entire company and the people around them that they live the company core values.

Here are some great pictures of pink unicorns all over the nation rocking their tracksuits on Tracksuit Thursday:

A lot of thought and creativity goes into bringing the core values to life in the organization using the core value swag. I encourage you to do this. This visual representation of the core values creates an environment where the core values are everywhere you look. The core values truly become the oxygen in the air, and no one even has to open their mouths or say them out loud for them to exist and manifest.

5. CORE VALUE COMMUNICATIONS AND AWARDS

Core values need to become the language of the organization. At TMS, we do not waste any opportunity to promote our core values. Especially when it comes to corporate communication. We use every chance we get to speak about our core values: corporate communication, company newsletters, wishing a team member a happy birthday, celebrating a work anniversary, and more. Our core values and pink unicorn mascot are painted across all these areas of the business. Our company newsletter was called the *Pink Unicorn Gazette* until we moved to a social platform that we named Unicornopolis to promote all our company communication. The idea is to take these symbols and ideas and use them where appropriate.

We have also built a company awards program, where we allow team members to nominate one another for any one of five areas:

- People Matter. Award
- Inspiring Leadership Award
- Strength of Character Award
- Rock Solid Service Award
- Pink Unicorn of the Year

Every person in the company has an opportunity to nominate team members who have exhibited the core value for the specific award. The team member must give details as to how this person embodies the core value they are being nominated for and why the nominee deserves this award. As a management team, we then look at the results and pick the winner. There are usually hundreds of nominees. However, we only select one or two winners per core value, which makes the award that much more special in our organization. Those who stand out but do not win an individual award may qualify for what we call a "Core Value Award."

This is basically an honorable mention. The Pink Unicorn of the Year is the person who stands out for more than one core value. Think of this as Team Member of the Year. This is like winning the Best Picture Oscar at our company. It is a huge deal and an enormous honor. The award winners get public recognition in front of the entire company and are treated to a beautiful dinner with the owners of the company. We get to have fun and spend time with each other in a meaningful way, celebrating their great work and commitment to living our core values at TMS. The idea is simple: create recognition around the core values. Get the team members to use them by nominating one another; then bring the core values to life by presenting meaningful awards whereby the team members get to feel pride and recognition for living the core values. It is truly special to see a team embrace core values in this way.

CONCLUSION

There are dozens, if not hundreds, of ways to bring core values to life in an organization. The examples in this chapter are things that have worked well for TMS and are best practices when it comes to taking an intangible idea like a core value and making it user-friendly, fun, and eventually sticky throughout your organization. My best piece of advice regarding the rollout of these initiatives goes back to the idea of *Tiny Habits*. Start small, roll out one initiative, and get the organization to do that one thing religiously until it becomes second nature (my definition of "second nature" is that if the person who manages it gets hit by a bus tomorrow, the initiative will live on). Then add another one. The points in this chapter are meant to be done in order, as you want to build on a strong foundation. Think of things you can do to make the core values come to life in your organization, and have fun with it. The goal is to bring the core values to life in a way that works for your organization.

HOW TO PROVE THAT CORE VALUES ARE NOT JUST FLUFF

If you are reading this book, there is a high likeliness that you believe that core values are an important part of scaling a business. Although I have met many people who are huge believers in this type of work, I have also met my fair share of critics and cynics who like to call this "fluff." In the world of business, expertise around finance, execution, operations, and getting things done is highly rewarded. Many managers who excel in these strengths and talents have sometimes not been introduced to the less tangible side of business and people management. I have seen this with leaders, coworkers, and even business partners who only begrudgingly agree to spend time on the culture and core values side of the business. I remember when I first introduced my business partner, Ali, to the idea of running a core-value-driven organization. He loved seeing that I was so into this way of running the business. My enthusiasm was contagious, but, at the same time, he called it fluff. Although he was a skeptic, he took a chance and is now one of my biggest supporters. His initial skepticism is shared by many people.

I was once having a conversation with a friend (let's call him Jason) around the culture of his company; he was running a successful logistics business. We were discussing how his team felt about their jobs. At the time, the company had about one hundred employees, had a couple of solid years of revenue growth, and was making money. On the surface, and to the uninformed, it looked like it was doing very well.

"So," I asked him, "do you think your employees love working for your company?"

"Well, yes—of course."

"How do you know?

"What do you mean, how do I know?" Jason said. "They work for us, don't they?"

"Well yeah, I see that—but how do you know they are engaged and giving you their all?"

"I just know."

I pushed him again. "How?"

"Because I know."

"What proof do you have?"

"My proof is they show up for work," he said. "And they should be happy just to have a job."

This is seriously how this conversation ended. The point I was trying to demonstrate to Jason—which is not where the conversation ended up—is best summed up by the famous words of Peter Drucker: **if you can't measure it, you can't improve it.** Jason and I were speaking different languages; he was having trouble wrapping his head around what I was asking him because he saw core values as fluff—as the *intangible* in an organization. When we think of culture and values as fluff, we don't give it the credit it deserves. We are assigning the label of "intangible" to something that can be made tangible when looked at from a different perspective. Culture and core values should be measured in the same way we measure anything else in organizations, such as profit and loss, or balance sheet equity, or cash flow. You should be able to measure how strong the core values are and how engaged your team is around the type of culture you have in place.

It is imperative to make the intangible **tangible** in your organization. This is the most effective way to get buy-in for your core values (from your co-founders, from your team, and from skeptics)—make these intangible ideas around culture more than just fluffy and touchy-feely words, mascots, and pink unicorns. Measure them. When we don't do this, we are simply guessing and using anecdotal information to make decisions. This is like running a business without looking at any KPIs, financial reports, or performance metrics. Obviously, this is not how you want to run the operations side of your business. Your culture and core values should be looked at in the same way.

The purpose of creating a core-value-driven organization is to create a high-performing company. One that wins. One that is superior to its peers. The idea that this is all just "fluff" is born from the notion that these things are promoted in an organization without the company's performance in mind. I admit, selfishly, that I do it for more than just creating high performance in my company. I do it because, as a CEO, leader, and entrepreneur, I build organizations and cultures that reflect the type of company I want to be a part of. With that said, I like to win, and I want to win. I believe that creating a core-value-driven organization is a great differentiator that allows me to win in my business. Teams are made up of people. I will fall on my sword until the end of time about the fact that people want to be part of something greater than themselves. The greatest empires, nations, armies, and organizations throughout history have proven this to be true. A strong culture is the glue that holds people together behind a common cause. The stronger the glue, the stronger the bond that the organization has. However, just saying this does not prove it to be true. The proof is in measuring the results of bringing the core values to life and nurturing them in the organization.

When we built our core values and culture at TMS, we started just as many of you will start. We started small and grew, step by step and brick by brick. This process is outlined in previous chapters. Once the core values were launched, we started to look at tools to measure how we were doing. We landed on a couple of key tools:

1. NPS and eNPS—Bain's loyalty tool
2. Q12—Gallup's engagement tool
3. Core Value Ratings
   A. Monthly Core Value Team Ratings
   B. Executive Quarterly Core Value Assessment

1. NPS AND ENPS

NPS stands for Net Promoter Score, and eNPS is Employee Net Promoter Score. NPS is a customer loyalty tool used by many Fortune 100 companies to see how loyal their customers are to their brand. eNPS is the same tool, only turned internally to see how loyal your team is to your company. Netpromoter.com defines NPS as follows:

> Net Promoter Score®, or NPS®, measures customer experience and predicts business growth. This proven metric transformed the business world and now provides the core measurement for customer experience management programs the world round.

% PROMOTERS — % DETRACTORS = NPS (NET PROMOTER SCORE

The NPS Calculation

Calculate your NPS using the answer to a key question, using a 0 to 10 scale: How likely is it that you would recommend [brand] to a friend or colleague?

Respondents are grouped as follows:

Promoters (score 9–10) are loyal enthusiasts who will keep buying and refer others, fueling growth.

Passives (score 7–8) are satisfied but unenthusiastic customers who are vulnerable to competitive offerings.

Detractors (score 0–6) are unhappy customers who can damage your brand and impede growth through negative word-of-mouth.

Subtracting the percentage of Detractors from the percentage of Promoters yields the Net Promoter Score, which can range from a low of –100 (if every customer is a Detractor) to a high of 100 (if every customer is a Promoter).[16]

The NPS and eNPS can be very volatile scores. However, they do provide a valuable benchmarking tool with which to measure an organization against outside organizations. This is supported by the prevalence of NPS/eNPS use around the world. Again, if you cannot measure it, you cannot improve it. If we are putting in the time, money, and investment into building a core-value-driven organization, it needs to be for the result of building a higher-performing company. NPS and eNPS communicate how an organization is performing, measuring not only against itself, but also against organizations worldwide. The reason I like to measure externally when looking at culture and core values is that I believe your customer experience directly correlates to how your people are performing inside the organization. If a company cares about its team and the leaders are leading the right way, then the team should be performing at higher levels that result in a great customer experience. Inversely, if there is inconsistency or things are broken in the organization, then your customer experience may suffer and that, too, will be reflected in your customer's experience. You will likely see NPS scores that reflect a less loyal customer.

At TMS, we measure our NPS monthly in every customer-facing department of the organization. This is a very quick way to

---

16 "What Is Net Promoter?" last modified 2017, Netpromoter.com.

diagnose issues in the business. If the score moves in a meaningful way, we know something is going on. This allows us to dig deeper into the business to see what is broken. Sometimes, it's simply a broken process that is already being fixed. Other times, it is a deeper issue, such as a misaligned manager who is bringing down a department's morale. This then trickles into the customer experience. Given how sensitive the NPS score is, it is a quick way to see if there are issues without having to wait too long. This also allows us to tangibly compare ourselves to the outside world. If we say we are better than the rest, it is not simply our opinion—rather, it is a concrete score that validates such a statement. NPS benchmark data can be found for most industries.

After we successfully rolled out NPS at TMS and began to see the NPS data and responses, we decided to turn inward and look at what our team had to say. This assessment is known as eNPS. eNPS is simply NPS turned inward, for employees. We started looking at this early on, as we believe that our first customer is our internal team. eNPS matters with regards to core values and cultural strength because eNPS measures loyalty. If you have built a core-value-driven organization, you should have a group of people who are more loyal to your company. This should hold true compared to a competitor who is not a core-value-driven organization. So, if you claim to have a rock-star culture but the eNPS says otherwise, then you may have issues regarding the execution, adoption, or maintenance of your core values.

You should be consistently monitoring the eNPS and NPS as early indicators of issues that need to be addressed in the company. If the scores are strong, then you are good to go—it is business as usual. For larger organizations, I recommend measuring by department, location, department by location, and as a whole. This provides very strong benchmarking data when you are comparing different departments and locations.

A median score will also start to emerge. This has allowed us to see issues in departments that were previously not so obvious. For instance, if I have a department in one location that scored a 45 eNPS and the same department in another location scored an 11 eNPS, I know something is wrong in the location with the 11 score. I also look at the company median score to see how the 11 compares. If the company score is 11, then the 11 in the one location is no longer an outlier; rather, the 45 score may be the outlier. It is important to benchmark the entire company before you start looking department by department.

At TMS we measure the eNPS quarterly. This has been a great tool to identify managerial issues in departments and locations in our business. It has also shown us when a new manager, location, or department has done a great job. I consider both equally import-ant. When a department or location is having issues, we have the team put together an action plan to tell us specifically what they are going to do to address the eNPS and NPS issues. When departments and locations are thriving, we have them share what is working for them with the entire organization, and we use this as a tool for struggling departments and locations. Many of our best practices at TMS have been adopted from this type of sharing.

Do not be discouraged or overconfident when you get low or high NPS and eNPS scores. NPS and eNPS are probably the most sensitive and volatile tools you will use in your company. As I like to say:

"The great thing about morale is that it changes very quickly. The worst thing about morale is that it changes very quickly."

When you are doing a great job, be vigilant and keep it up, as your NPS and eNPS can nose-dive very quickly. When you are doing poorly, do not be discouraged, as they can improve dramatically overnight. It all starts with building the foundation for a great customer experience, which lies directly in having and maintaining a core-value-driven organization. Your customers will tell you exactly how you are doing in this regard, both internally and externally. All you have to do is provide them with the opportunity to be vocal and not be afraid to listen.

2. Q^{12}

The Q^{12} is Gallup's employee engagement tool. In our quarterly cultural survey, we started asking the Q^{12} questions to our team. The Q^{12} is a more tactical tool that shows if your team is engaged or not. Our perspective is that if the core values are alive and well within your organization, then you should have a team of engaged individuals supporting your company and customers. At TMS, we built a strengths-based organization that focuses on employee engagement. The tool we used for this is Gallup's CliftonStrengths, which we love and promote within our organization. We wanted to measure our culture and core values in meaningful ways to get away from the idea that this is all just fluff that cannot be quantified. I was introduced to the Q^{12} by our CliftonStrengths coach and ran with it in our organization early on. Here is some background on the Q^{12} tool directly from Gallup:

> Gallup researchers spent decades writing and testing hundreds of questions, because their wording and order mean everything when it comes to accurately measuring engagement. Their research yielded Gallup's Q^{12} survey: the 12 questions that measure the most important elements of employee engagement.

Gallup has studied survey results from more than 35 million employees around the world. We wrote the bestselling book on engagement—twice. All of our research points to one thing:

Gallup's Q^{12} survey is the most effective measure of employee engagement and its impact on the outcomes that matter most to your business.

Measurement That Means Something:

Employees answer 12 simple questions, available in over 30 languages including Arabic, Chinese, Spanish, French, German **and more**, that tie directly to performance outcomes.

Scores are on a 1 to 5 scale, which clearly highlights strengths and opportunities.

When improvement efforts focus on the essential elements of engagement, those measured by the Q^{12} survey, team performance [improves.][17]

The twelve questions that we ask our team on a quarterly basis are as follows:

1. Do you know what is expected of you at work?
2. Do you have the materials and equipment to do your work right?
3. At work, do you have the opportunity to do what you do best every day?
4. In the last seven days, have you received recognition or praise for doing good work?

---

17 "Gallup Q^{12} Employee Engagement Survey," Gallup, last modified 2016, https://q12.gallup.com/public/en-us/Features.

5. Does your supervisor, or someone at work, seem to care about you as a person?
6. Is there someone at work who encourages your development?
7. At work, do your opinions seem to count?
8. Does the mission/purpose of your company make you feel your job is important?
9. Are your associates (fellow employees) committed to doing quality work?
10. Do you have a best friend at work?
11. In the last six months, has someone at work talked to you about your progress?
12. In the last year, have you had opportunities to learn and grow?

We then have the team score each question from 1 to 5 based on the following answers:

- 5—Strongly Agree
- 4—Agree
- 3—Neutral
- 2—Disagree
- 1—Strongly Disagree

After we get the results, we calculate the score per question and the overall score. This is the average of all twelve questions' scores. Just as we look at the entire organization, we also dissect the final scores by department, by location, and by department by location. The results show a median score for these different data points, as well as outliers or areas of improvement to shoot for.

After doing the Q^{12} in our organization for many years, I have learned a few things. The score you want to shoot for is an overall score of 4.2 or higher out of a possible score of 5. I notice we are doing our best when our team scores at 4.2 or higher. The difference between 4.1 and 4.2 is profound. As is the difference between 4.0 and 4.1. When we have dipped below 4.0, it means we have some serious issues we need to work on. The thing I love most about the Q^{12} is that it gives direct insights into what we can do to improve. For instance, if our score on the following question is low:

Do you have the materials and equipment to do your work right?

I can dig into what materials or equipment the team is lacking to do their job better and fix it right away.

If I see an issue on the following question:

In the last six months, has someone at work talked to you about your progress?

I can meet with the HR team and make sure we have formalized one-on-ones to discuss career tracking in our organization.

The Q^{12} is very specific in showing us areas in which we need to improve to create and maintain an engaged workforce. It goes without saying that an engaged workforce supports a superior organization. The data around this are profound:

According to Gallup, organizations with highest performers have three things going for them:

(1) they have tenures of a decade or more in their organizations

(2) they are engaged in their work and

(3) they are in roles where the expectations of the job align well with their innate talents. Each variable affects outcomes on its own, but the highest performance comes from the combination.

When your organization focuses on employee engagement and satisfaction, it not only attracts quality talent for your company but also helps you retain your existing employees better.

Employee productivity is important to any business. The more productive your employees are, the more successful you'll be as a business. According to Gallup, highly engaged teams are 21% more productive and have 28% less internal theft than those with low engagement. Engaged employees are innovative and always have an idea or two about what they can do better. Their quality of being collaborative and enthusiastic toward work, allows them to complete their workplace goals more effectively; which leads to increased workplace productivity.[18]

It goes without saying that employee engagement matters. We measure this the same way we measure profitability in our company, as we know that 21 percent more productivity equals profit. A couple of things to keep in mind when measuring your Q^{12}:

1. We measure this anonymously on a quarterly basis across our entire organization.
2. If we have soft spots in a department or location or a specific department in a specific office, then we have them build an accountability plan for the coming quarter. If there is

---

18 "The Impact of Employee Engagement on Productivity," Engagedly, August 8, 2018, https:// engagedly.com/impact-of-employee-engagement-on-productivity/.

no specific plan to fix something, then we can't expect a different result in the future.

3. The Q12 is far less volatile than the eNPS or NPS. The managers and leadership have much more control over the Q12 results than the eNPS results. I have had huge downward swings in our eNPS because we sold a business or had to deal with a reduction in force or made a strategic decision that made our team uneasy about referring friends to work at the company (eNPS). Simultaneously, I have seen record-high Q12 scores because we as an organization were doing all the right things in supporting our team and running a great company. To me, the Q12 is the most important score in the company. I believe this to be true when it comes to measuring the engagement of our team. I firmly believe this happens when our core values are thriving in our organization and we are doing the right things for our people.

Here is Q^{12} data aggregated at TMS in the recent years:

Q12 QUESTION	Q1 18'	Q2 18'	Q3 18'	Q1 19'	Q2 19'	Qtr Var	YTD AVG
I know what is expected of me at work.	4.51	4.44	4.45	4.50	4.40	-0.11	4.45
I have the materials and equipment I need to do my work right.	4.19	4.19	4.20	4.16	4.01	-0.15	4.09
At work, I have the opportunity to do what I do best everyday.	4.28	4.22	4.22	4.24	4.16	-0.09	4.20
In the last seven days, I have received recognition or praise for doing good work.	4.08	4.12	4.03	4.07	3.98	-0.08	4.03
My supervisor, or someone at work, seems to care about me as a person.	4.44	4.42	4.46	4.49	4.45	-0.05	4.47
There is someone at work who encourages my development.	4.26	4.25	4.19	4.26	4.18	-0.09	4.22
At work, my opinions seem to count.	3.99	3.99	3.97	4.08	3.88	-0.20	3.99
The mission or purpose of my company makes me feel my job is important.	4.28	4.20	4.15	4.15	4.00	-0.14	4.08
My associates or fellow employees are committed to doing quality work.	4.25	4.25	4.34	4.30	4.11	-0.19	4.21
I have a best friend at work.	3.63	3.59	3.58	3.66	3.62	-0.05	3.64
In the last 6 months, someone at work has talked to me about my progress.	4.14	4.06	3.95	4.35	4.10	-0.25	4.23
This last year, I have had the opportunites at work to learn and grow.	4.13	4.14	4.07	4.26	4.06	-0.20	4.17
Average	4.18	4.16	4.13	4.21	4.08	-0.13	4.15

As you can see from this spreadsheet, the scores on the Q^{12} tend to be rather stable. As I mentioned earlier, scores under 4.2 tend to indicate an area for improvement. The only exception to this is the BFAW (pronounced BO-FA), which stands for Best Friend at Work question, which I have found tends to be in the mid-three range.

Conversely, when I look at the eNPS data for TMS, I see wide and varying scores by location and by quarter:

eNPS by Location

Office	Q4 16'	Q1 17'	Q2 17'	Q3 17'	Q4 17'	Q1 18'	Q2 18'	Q3 18'	Q1 19'
Office 1	39.1%	17.6%	18.2%	25.9%	42.9%	35.5%	29.2%	26.6%	12.0%
Office 2	44.1%	18.9%	12.9%	30.3%	28.6%	22.9%	41.2%	26.1%	9.1%
Office 3	43.6%	21.8%	40.4%	41.1%	66.1%	53.4%	42.2%	46.7%	37.5%
Office 4	53.3%	46.2%	15.3%	25.8%	24.6%	25.3%	36.2%	48.2%	54.0%
Office 5	31.8%	44.8%	45.2%	63.3%	62.2%	50.0%	56.7%	45.5%	52.6%
Office 6	6.8%	39.8%	67.9%	58.3%	87.5%	66.7%	10.5%	16.7%	20.0%
Office 7	41.8%	26.1%	6.9%	8.1%	42.5%	35.5%	29.2%	16.6%	12.0%
Office 8	8.8%	29.0%	39.1%	17.5%	4.9%	25.7%	42.8%	36.2%	29.2%
Total eNPS	33.0%	28.6%	26.4%	36.4%	52.9%	40.6%	49.9%	37.4%	31.1%

Both tools are useful and powerful when used appropriately and consistently in an organization. I see this as an unbiased way to measure the effectiveness of our core value work in building a more engaged workforce that is loyal to our company. We measure the effectiveness of this work in our organization in the same way we measure revenue, expenses, profitability, KPIs, and so on. Over the years, there have been many times when I have seen issues pop up on our NPS, eNPS, and Q^{12}. Sometimes, this would occur in the company and sometimes it was much more specific—in a department, location, or even as specific as a singular department in a singular location. When I have shown these results to my business partner, who manages the operations side of the business, ten times out of ten there are issues showing up in more traditional measurements of operational concern. These might include productivity KPIs suffering, financial KPIs underperforming, or departmental turnover.

The opposite is true when I see very strong eNPS and Q^{12} data. When those scores are doing very well, I see that these areas of the business are thriving, both from a productivity and financial profitability standpoint. From these experiences, I have become a true believer that implementing cultural assessment tools such as the Q^{12}, NPS, and eNPS are akin to taking one's blood pressure, measuring heart rate, or testing blood—these are the company's vitals. When these are good, the company is healthy. However, if something does not look right, attention needs to be quickly paid to what is wrong and how to fix it. Ignoring this will likely cause much bigger issues in the future.

The key takeaways on NPS, eNPS, and Q^{12} are the following:

- NPS should be done monthly by each line of business. It should represent how your customers feel about the product and service you are providing. The scores are a direct reflection of the organization you are running. Lower scores may not be a cultural issue, but rather a broken process. If your scores are not where you want them to be, you may want to ask yourself the following question: *what do your core values say you need to do to provide a great customer experience, and why is this not happening?* In a core-value-driven organization, the fix should already be in place when you see the lower score and should already be happening. If this is not the case in your organization, then you have work to do.
- eNPS and Q^{12} should be measured in an anonymous survey

once a quarter. This is your internal report card. At TMS, we measure this by location, department, and location by department.

- Pull eNPS and NPS benchmark data from credible sources online. Scores tend to shift by industry and by job duties.
- A score of 4.2 or above is the goal for you in terms of overall and individual Q^{12} scores. If you are below 4.2, you have work to do. Mid-three range is acceptable for the BFAW question.

3. CORE VALUE RATINGS

The entire premise of this chapter is the idea of measuring the intangible. To many in the business world, the idea of "culture" and "core values" is fluff that HR folks use to justify their jobs. With core values, there is a baseline set of beliefs that should justify every decision, action, and result in the organization. Let's go back to our results equation from earlier in the book:

CORE VALUES = DECISIONS = ACTIONS = RESULTS

The goal is to create an organization that eats, sleeps, breathes, and lives the core values at all times. I have outlined dozens of methods not only to create and bring the core values to life in your organization, but also to keep them alive and well in the organization. I've also outlined tools to indirectly measure how well the core values are doing, through measuring customer experience, employee engagement, and so on (NPS, eNPS, Q^{12}). But there are also ways to directly measure how alive and well the core values are in your organization. I recommend:

A. Monthly Core Value Team Ratings
B. Executive Quarterly Core Value Assessment

A. MONTHLY CORE VALUE TEAM RATINGS

There are multiple ways to conduct these ratings in an organization, and this usually depends on the size of the company. For organizations under twenty people, the best practice is to have a monthly all-hands meeting. This meeting is a great opportunity to have a core value rating exercise. The core value exercise is as follows:

1. Each month, pick one core value. Have a team member read the core value header and descriptive out loud in front of the entire team.
2. After the team member is done reading the core value, give the team a few minutes to score how alive and well the core value is in the organization as of this moment. The scores should be on a scale of 1 to 10. A score of 1 means that core value is not alive and well in the organization. A score of 10 means the core value could not be more alive and well in the organization.
3. After the team has had a few minutes to write down their scores, go around the room and have everyone share their score and why they gave the score. This is a great opportunity to learn about how the team feels things are going in the organization. It also creates the opportunity for the team to use the core values as the language of the organization together in a conversation.

Use this opportunity to narrate, using the core values as the language of the story. This is how real learning is done. It sets the precedent that the leadership of the organization truly cares about the core values and uses them as a standard for the organization above all else. I recommend that this be done first thing in your all-hands meeting.

For organizations greater than twenty people, this can become very time-consuming. I recommend integrating this into monthly team surveying and then sharing the results with your managers monthly. This can work at scale when done in this format. It is not quite as strong as having one-on-one conversations as a team, but it is another touchpoint using the core values as a standard for behavior and accountability in your organization.

I have also had teams score the core values once a month in their team huddles. The goal here is to have an empirical score tied to how alive and well the core values are in the organization.

B. EXECUTIVE QUARTERLY CORE VALUE ASSESSMENT

Our executive team meets every quarter to do our quarterly strategic planning. If you are not doing this, you can introduce this concept into your executive manager meeting once a month. I recommend that you roll this out with your senior leadership team on either a monthly or quarterly basis.

At TMS, we do this rating at our quarterly strategic meeting and use it as an icebreaker to kick off the meetings. In our strategic meeting, we do it slightly different than we described above, in that we do all four of our core values. The concept is the same in that the team is discussing, rating, and assessing the organization from the vantage point of the core values. We have four volunteers on the team read the core values out loud. We then score the core values on the scale of 1 to 10. After we score each core value, we go around the room, give our score, and discuss why we gave that score for the specific core value. We then move to the next core value until we get through all of our core values as a group. This has become programmed into our organization. It has become a consistent opportunity to hold the company and leaders accountable to the core values. It demonstrates to the highest leaders in the organization that the core values are the most important standard by which we hold ourselves accountable as an organization.

When programmed into an organization in the ways described in this chapter, we set the precedent and give our team the ability to use the language of the core values. This is done from the perspective of what matters most to the organization. This exercise is a game-changer and will take your core values and accountability regarding the core values to levels you cannot imagine.

CONCLUSION

To reiterate, the cadence I have outlined in this chapter is as follows:

NPS—This should be assessed monthly with your clients. This gives an insight into how loyal your customers are to your organization. I believe this is one data point to show whether your core values are alive and well in an organization. If the team is doing a great job and treating the customer well, then the NPS should reflect this.

eNPS—This should be assessed on a quarterly basis through direct employee surveying. This is done best in an anonymous environment, as people tend to be most transparent and honest when they feel the risk is low. Be sure to ask your team the following question after you have them rate the company:

Why did you give us this score? If you did not score us a 10, what could we do to score a 10 in the future?

You will be amazed at the verbatim answers that come from this question.

Q^{12}—Use the same anonymous survey that you use for the eNPS and include the Q^{12}. As I mention in this chapter, this is probably the most valuable tool you will have to measure your team's engagement in your organization. I love the Q^{12} assessment. If your scores are not where you want them to be, I recommend having each leader bring the relevant Q^{12} question(s) into their team's monthly one-on-ones. This will give them three months to address these concerns and work on weak areas before the next quarterly assessment.

Core value ratings—This should be done monthly, either in person or via a monthly survey with the team. In person is always best; however, with larger teams, this is not scalable and you will need to use your pulse surveying to ask the question. Share the results with your managers if done via survey. With the senior management team, I recommend doing one core value face-to-face per month in your monthly leadership meeting, or do all four or five core values as an icebreaker at your quarterly strategic meeting.

Peter Drucker once said his now-famous quote: "If you can't measure it, you can't improve it." When we treat our core values and culture as an investment in the strength and performance of the organization, we approach them from a completely different angle than if we were just doing it because we think people will "like it" or it's what we're supposed to do. Treat this like you would any large investment in your organization: with care, intentionality, respect, and accountability. I promise you, the return on your investment will exceed your wildest expectations.

CONCLUSION

THE LANGUAGE OF YOUR ORGANIZATION

In the fall of 2018, I had the great honor of working with acclaimed performance coach David Zelman, of the Transitions Institute (www.transitionsinstitute.com). David has a four-month coaching course called the Transitions Program. The Transitions Program is a unique program directed at peak performance and leveling up as a leader. In my case, we worked on self-management and my abilities to take my game as a leader to the next level. It was truly an eye-opening experience, and David is a genius when it comes to the work he has done in this area. If you get the opportunity, I highly recommend checking out this program and his work.

During the Transitions Program, I had an epiphany with David that connected all the dots for me when it came to core values and their impact on our lives and organizations we lead. In our third month of working together, David asked me an interesting question. He said, "Darius, how do you think it is that you get the results that you want in the world? How do results happen?" My first guess was simple: "Well, do they happen because of the actions that we take?" But David pushed me further: "Okay, what creates the actions that we take?" I started taking guesses ("Are they things that you think and things you do?"), and David kept probing me and moving me along. I kept guessing wrong. At one point, I was nine guesses in and not landing any of my answers. Finally, I gave up and David gave me the answer. He said, "Well, what if it was the conversations that we have with ourselves?"

I could really see that. We, as humans, have thousands of conversations with ourselves every day. Based on this, David and I worked on the following equation which I interpreted as follows:[19]

CONVERSATIONS = DECISIONS = ACTIONS = RESULTS

The number of decisions (aka choices) we make daily is staggering. A *Psychology Today* article from September 2018 offers the following data:

"In fact, some sources suggest that the average person makes an eye-popping 35,000 choices per day. Assuming that most people spend around seven hours per day sleeping and thus blissfully choice-free, that makes roughly 2,000 decisions per hour or one decision every two seconds."[20]

If we are making two thousand decisions per hour or thirty-five thousand per day, how many conversations are we having

19   David Zelman, *If I Can, You Can: Transformation Made Easy* (Tucson: Wheatmark, 2016), 26–30.

20   Eva M. Krockow, "How Many Decisions Do We Make Each Day?" *Psychology Today*, September 27, 2018, https://www.psychologytoday.com/us/blog/stretching-theory/201809/how-many-decisions-do-we-make-each-day.

to come to those decisions? At least thirty-five thousand—but likely more, given the nature of how decisions are made. My conversations usually look something like this: *Oh, should I eat that pizza, should I not eat that pizza? Should I go work out, should I not work out? Do I want to pick up my shoe, yes or no? Do I really want to yell at my son? Do I want to watch this movie? Man, I can't believe that guy drove like that; I'm going to make a left over here.* From these thousands of conversations we have with ourselves per day, we commit to thousands of actions and, from that, we end up with thousands of results. These numbers and this concept are pretty mind-blowing when we quantify and think about our lives in these terms.

Around two months after I finished the Transitions Program, I had a follow-up call with David—a post-mortem, if you will. I shared with him what I had realized:

"David, I've had an epiphany about your transitions process. I have been thinking a lot about the Transitions Program, especially about the equation you taught me

CONVERSATIONS = DECISIONS = ACTIONS = RESULTS

But I realize that there's one step further that I want to take this. What are our conversations made up of? They are made up of language and words."

If our core values are the words and language of our organizations, then it should be easy to surmise that they become the building blocks for the conversations of our organizations. Using David Zelman's equation, this would mean that they lead to the *results* in our organizations. The words we use build the conversations that we have, which lead to the decisions we make, which create the actions, which lead to our results. Put simply:

CORE VALUES = WORDS = CONVERSATIONS = DECISIONS = ACTIONS = RESULTS

From this, you can see that every result in our organization is a direct result of the company's core values. If we want to control the results, we must control the core values.

I have distilled this into the Core Value Equation we saw in the book:

CORE VALUES = DECISIONS = ACTIONS = RESULTS

It was a beautiful moment for me to realize that the work I had been doing over the past fifteen years was not just cultural fluff. The rubber was meeting the road when I connected the dots with the Transitions Program. If you want to control the results, you must first control the conversations and, since conversations are made up of language, you must control the words. The core values are the words and language of the organization and of our lives. They are the foundation of every outcome we will ever experience. Control the words and you control the conversations; control the conversations and you control the results. I am more bullish now than ever about this idea. It all starts with our core values. Core values = results. When the core values are discovered, designed, managed, adopted, and brought to life, they become the language by which we manage ourselves, our organizations, our families, and our communities. When this happens, we can determine the results we want from our lives.

My hope is that this book will help you create a roadmap for how to discover and design an authentic set of core values for your organization. When this is done well, you can build a language for your organizations that enables you to build the company of your dreams. Control the language and you will control the results. This is truly a representation that words matter.

The questions I leave you with are simple: *What language and words are being spoken in your organizations? Are you and your team having the conversations that eventually lead to the results you are looking for?* I empower you to take control of the language and conversations that happen in your organizations and your life. This starts with the core values. I hope this book has given you the tools to create a core-value-driven organization that embodies what you wish for and deserve.

Thank you for taking the time to read this. It's been my great honor to share this information with you, and I am looking forward to seeing more core-value-driven organizations create change and impact in our world.

Earning your Pink Unicorn Tracksuit

Why a tracksuit? The Pink Unicorn Tracksuit signifies the hard work and dedication of a fellow Pink Unicorn. It is earned by those team members who exhibit strength of character, rock solid service, and that simple motive and/or inspiring leadership. It is a symbol of a team member who has gone above and beyond and embodies high performance. Something that all aspire to and proudly wear.

The history of the tracksuit goes back to when Dellos was...

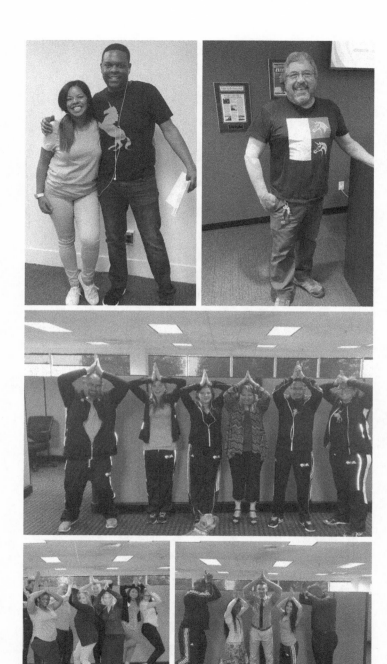

ACKNOWLEDGMENTS

Writing this book has been one of the most inspirational and creative things I have ever done. It is the culmination of the past 16 years of my work attempting to build a great company. There have been many lessons learned along the way and many people who have contributed to what has become the content in this book.

I want to start by thanking my business partners Mike, Ali, and Stavros. Our company TMS has been one great big experiment for my mad science and I am eternally grateful for your trust, encouragement and support. I could never have learned all that I have learned in order to write this book if it was not for your support and us building our company together. I appreciate you all more than you will ever know.

I want to thank Ken Sims and John DeHart. The workshop you two led at BOG was a pivotal turning point in my life. It was an eye-opening experience which became the catalyst for my work for these next 11 years. I am very grateful for your wisdom. Thank you for that moment in 2008.

I want to thank my dear friend Summer Thommen. Much of my work was inspired by work that we did together and your amazing intuition. You have inspired me and you have been a very important part of the design process for much of our core value creative process and core value roll out. I am extremely thankful for our debates and conversations regarding the subject of core values and there is no doubt in my mind that this book would not be what it is without the time and energy that we have spent working on our company core values, onboarding process and ongoing support. You are incredible and more amazing than you know.

I want to thank the one and only Dr. David Zelman. Our work together really connected the dots for me in ways that I could never have imagined. You are on a different level my friend. Your work has been life changing for me and has truly created a foundation by which I am better able to understand myself and my work when it comes to core values and the results we have in our life. The title of this book is dedicated to you and our work that we have done together. I cannot tell you how meaningful this has been for me and what it has done for my work on this subject. There is not enough thanks I can give for where this has brought me to.

I want to thank my beta readers Darra Landman, Jeff Schox, Ali Vafai, Maria Coh Prospero, and my lovely wife Maria. You all gave me great notes which made this a better book. I truly appreciate the time and energy you took. Although it made the editing process longer than I had hoped. It made this book the best that it could be and for that I am forever grateful.

Lastly, I want to thank two very important people in my life.

Mom, you have been an inspiration on living a life that is driven by your values. You are an amazing human being. Your love of reading and talent for writing planted the seed for me at the youngest of ages with regard to writing my own book. I know this part of me comes directly from you. I am grateful for everything you have ever done for me.

Maria, you have been my biggest supporter and rock for all of these years. The trials and tribulations of my entrepreneurial life have always had you there to support me. You are an amazing life partner and I know without question that this book would not have come to be if I did not have you and your support. I love you very much and I am more grateful than you will ever know to have you in my life.

APPENDIX

INSPIRING LEADERSHIP POLICY AND PROCEDURES

Being a leader at The Money Source Inc. (TMS) requires that we **ARE** the example of what the organization stands for. Every action, behavior, comment, and employee interaction is reflective of the Core Values of the organization to its core. How we carry ourselves, how we treat our team members, how we speak to each other and to everyone in the organization, all the way down to how we present ourselves via dress code, the way we sit at our desk, and the tone we carry in our voices defines to our team whether or not we are a leader, let alone an inspirational leader. For this reason it is imperative that we be the example within the organization and live the core values. In order to do so, we must take the following actions:

LEADING FROM THE FRONT LINES!

- Temperature Check with your direct reports on a daily basis (some hourly).

- Assess their workload and the morale of themselves and their team.
- If Direct Report is overwhelmed, assess if it is one of the following:
  - Time management issue
  - Workload issue, not enough bandwidth
  - System issue

A) TIME MANAGEMENT ISSUE

1. Coach and counsel direct report; manage them up to their highest ability.
2. Work on time management issues they may be running into.
3. Give your teammate direct roadmap on areas to streamline within their time management.
4. Step in and take load off teammate's plate when the teammate is not able to load balance or create excess bandwidth.

B) WORKLOAD

1. Work on workload issues they may be running into.
2. Give your teammate direct roadmap on areas to streamline within their time management.
3. Step in and take load off teammate's plate when the teammate is not able to load balance or create excess bandwidth.
4. Prioritize workload. What must happen today, and what can wait till tomorrow?

C) SYSTEM ISSUE

1. See if you can solve the issue with a small fix (workaround if known issue).
2. Is the problem isolated or system-wide?

3. Escalate to senior management team in management meeting to solve at 30,000-foot level.
4. If you can solve it, make sure your direct manager signs off on change.

GET INTO THE TRENCHES!

Although we want our teammates to live a balanced life, sometimes duty calls. Top Level management, specifically in the SVP and higher roles, are expected to get into the trenches when necessary. This means the following: HELPING our teammates when they need us, and preferably without them asking. We must be intuitive and proactive to try to figure out their needs ahead of schedule when possible.

HOW TO BE THE EXAMPLE AT TMS

To be the example at TMS, leadership must set the example to the team in the following areas:

1. Accessibility—We must always make ourselves accessible to our teammates so that they feel as though they can depend on us when they need us; we must be their crutch in times of need.
2. Communication—We must be quick and transparent. Our responsiveness must be excellent. We must be the embodiment of ROCK SOLID COMMUNICATION.
3. Approachability—We must give off a vibe of approachability; our team must trust us to be able to solve their problems.
4. Giving Recognition to Our Teammates—Remember that the second word in *Cheerleader* is LEADER. We are the Cheerleaders of TMS, so put on your pom-poms and shower your team with recognition.

COACHING AND TEACHING THE TEAM

To be an inspirational leader at TMS we must be the student and the teacher with our teams. In order to do so, we must listen to our team's needs and educate our teams so that they are continually growing and learning within the organization to become better teammates. Leaders in the organization are expected to produce at least one Rock Solid Training per month to your direct reports. These are to be led and created by different leaders within the organization per month. Each manager is expected to produce and lead three training subjects per quarter to the executive team.

INSPIRATIONAL LEADERSHIP ACCOUNTABILITY

It is imperative that leaders at TMS understand that we are 100 percent accountable for everything that goes on under our watch. Every person that reports to you all the way down to the bottom of the organization is a representation of your leadership. We own everything and everyone within our silo of management. As managers we are expected to take the bullets for our team and to promote their successes.

- TEAM = owns the wins
- LEADER = owns the failures

Given the above, we must fix every failure in a time-sensitive manner and guarantee that mistakes only occur once under our watch as we are expected to be proactive problem solvers.

INSPIRING LEADERSHIP TEAM HIRING AND TEAM TERMINATION

At TMS, we understand that every job is a livelihood, and

behind that job is a person who is working hard to support their family. These livelihoods build dreams, and we take the responsibility of the livelihood very seriously. As leaders we own the livelihoods of all of those that we represent at TMS. For this reason, we take great care and the necessary time to hire the right teammates. We understand that losing a teammate through termination can be a huge culture killer. For this reason, as well as our respect for each individual's livelihood, we take special care and as much time as needed to make sure that we are recruiting and eventually hiring the right teammates for TMS.

We also understand that unfortunately sometimes the wrong fits may have to go, as this is the only way we can guarantee the integrity of the culture of the organization. Leaders recognize that this is a balance and our leadership must take special care to maintain the balance at our company.

INSPIRATIONAL CULTURE OF HELPING

At TMS, we expect teammates to step up and help one another proactively. We also need to ask for help when we need it. If we need to bring on more staff to facilitate getting the job done, ask for more staff from your manager. If we need to bring in a temp for a short-term project, ask your manager for this opportunity. We must all get into the habit of asking for help proactively, as this is one of the pillars of teamwork.

CREATING THE PERFECT EXPERIENCE

As leaders at TMS, we must understand that the organization is striving to create the perfect customer experience. The only way this is possible is through:

- Inspecting what we expect
- Diligently analyzing the systems
- Proactively looking into the areas we are weak in
- Having an open mind
- Listening to our teams when they voice their concerns

We must be solutions-oriented at all times when building and fixing our systems, policies, and procedures.

INSPIRING LEADERSHIP STATURE

As leaders at TMS, we must carry ourselves and present ourselves as examples within the organization.

How do we do this?

1. Stand tall and proud.
2. Speak softly and respectfully at all times.
3. Maintain positive respectful tone in our emails and conversations.
4. Sit up straight with confidence.
5. Follow our dress code.
6. Use our physical presence as a symbol of all of our core values.
7. Speak with a smile in our voice.
8. Maintain an air of approachability in our demeanor.

ABOUT THE AUTHOR

DARIUS MIRSHAHZADEH is a high growth CEO, serial entrepreneur, and culture building mad scientist who was ranked #9 on Glassdoor's list of Top CEOs of Small and Medium Companies in the US. He's led organizations that have won numerous Stevie awards, been named "#3 Best Place to Work" by *San Francisco* Business *Times,* and have landed at #40 on the Inc. 500 list of fastest-growing companies. Darius has been recognized in the *New York Times* and *Inc. Magazine* for innovation in corporate culture, and his business insights and thought leadership have been published in *Huffington Post*, Entrepreneur.com, *Fast Company*, and *Forbes*.

Visit Darius online at www.therealdarius.com.

CPSIA information can be obtained
at www.ICGtesting.com
Printed in the USA
LVHW090553310520
656416LV00003B/3/J